Festive and Novelty Cakes

Festive and Novelty Cakes

MEREHURST PRESS
LONDON

Published 1987 by Merehurst Press
5 Great James Street
London WC1N 3DA

© Copyright 1987 Merehurst Limited

ISBN 0 948075 58 9

Managing Editor: Joyce Becker
Editor: Jane Struthers
Designer: Roger Daniels
Photographer: Graham Tann
Data conversion and phototypesetting:
Lineage Ltd, Watford
Colour separation:
Fotographics Ltd, London–Hong Kong
Printed in Belgium by Henri Proost, Turnhout, Belgium.

Contributors

Recipes devised and tested by Mary Cadogan

Cakes created and decorated by Dolly Meers,
Brenda Purton, Jenny Ridgwell, Ann Tann and
Jenny Walker

Acknowledgements

The Publishers wish to thank the following for
their help and advice:

Lucy Baker
Kim Golding
Rachel and Katy Tann

The Covent Garden General Store,
107-115 Long Acre, Covent Garden, London WC2N 4BA

Elizabeth David Ltd
46 Bourne Street, London SW1W 8JD
and at Covent Garden Kitchen Supplies,
3 North Row, The Market, Covent Garden, London WC2

B R Mathews & Son
12 Gipsy Hill, Upper Norwood, London SE19 1NN

A Piece of Cake,
18 Upper High Street, Thame, Oxfordshire OX9 2XE

Woodnutt's Ltd
97 Church Road, Hove, East Sussex BN3 2BA

Important: use only one set of measurements.
The quantities given in metric are not always exact
conversions of the imperial measurements.
Cup conversions of imperial measurements are
given below.

Imperial	Cups
¼ pint liquid	⅔ cup
½ pint liquid	1¼ cups
1 pint liquid	2½ cups
2 pints liquid	5 cups
1lb granulated or caster (superfine) sugar	2 cups
1lb brown sugar	2 cups
1lb icing (confectioner's) sugar	3½ cups
1lb butter	2 cups
1lb flour	4 cups
1lb dried fruit	3 cups
8oz glacé cherries	1 cup
4oz chopped nuts	1 cup
4oz cocoa powder	1 cup
1oz flour	¼ cup
1oz granulated or caster (superfine) sugar	2 tablespoons
1oz butter	2 tablespoons

CONTENTS

INTRODUCTION

A special celebration cake makes every festive occasion more exciting, and the person who can produce an original decorated cake will always be popular. *Festive and Novelty Cakes* has been designed particularly for newcomers to the art of cake decoration, or people who may only make a few cakes each year, but nevertheless want them to be impressive. The book contains precise instructions for thirty cakes, complete with all the information on the techniques needed to make each one. And since time is an important factor in everyone's life, all the cakes have been designed so that they can be decorated in one hour or less.

Festive and Novelty Cakes begins with a section on how to bake different types of cakes and how to make perfect icing. There are illustrated instructions for making and using piping bags; marzipanning and covering fruit cakes; icing sponges; and different ideas for using purchased cakes and decorations. All of the recipes have been devised and tested by a home economist, ensuring that each decorated cake will have a delicious base.

The thirty decorated cakes feature new ideas for every occasion – birthdays, anniversaries, weddings, christenings, Easter and Christmas, plus ideas for adapting the designs to different occasions. There are also some very unusual suggestions for decorating party sandwiches, pizzas and breads, plus suggestions for making cakes look spectacular without icing. The ten birthday cakes are all quick and easy to do, bearing in mind that parents of small children have very little spare time. Some of the special occasion cakes require a bit more time, but the clear instructions in the book make even these well within everyone's ability.

Festive and Novelty Cakes was created by a team of people who all enjoy cake decoration and sharing ideas on how to make wonderful cakes in a short space of time. Thanks to the home economist, Mary Cadogan, and the cake decorators themselves – Dolly Meers, Brenda Purton, Jenny Ridgwell, Ann Tann and Jenny Walker. Thanks also to the photographer, Graham Tann, designer, Roger Daniels and editor, Jane Struthers.

Joyce Becker

JOYCE BECKER
Managing Editor

EQUIPMENT

It is surprising how little equipment you need to make a wide variety of cakes. Much of it you may already have, and the rest can be built up gradually, as your skills and enthusiasm increase. Whatever you decide to buy, it is worthwhile choosing good-quality tins (pans) and utensils which will last. Tins made from firm metal will keep their shape even after years of use. Loose-based or springform tins are useful for removing cakes which are easily damaged, such as whisked sponges. Here is a list of basic equipment.

Mixing bowls of various sizes
500-ml (1-pint) measuring jug
Standard spoon measures
Nylon sieve
Wooden spoons – keep two or three
especially for cake-making
Plastic or rubber spatula
Large and small palette knife
Fine skewers
Fine string
Rolling pin
Greaseproof, waxed and non-stick paper
Aluminium foil

Icing nozzles
Choose metal rather than plastic nozzles for the best effects. If you are planning to pipe with royal icing, you should start with a medium writing nozzle, two sizes of star nozzle and perhaps a shell and petal nozzle. These small metal nozzles are usually fitted into greaseproof paper piping bags that you can easily make yourself. When piping buttercream and cream, you will need a larger metal tube, fitted into a cloth or plastic piping bag.

Tins (pans)
The following list gives you a useful selection of sizes and shapes for most needs. Build up your collection gradually, buying tins (pans) as and when you need them. As you develop your cake-making skills, you may want to acquire special tins, in the shape of numbers, hearts, horseshoes and so on. Many of these are available from large department stores, kitchen shops or by post from specialist suppliers.

17.5-cm (7-in) round deep cake tin
20-cm (8-in) round deep cake tin
2 17.5-cm (7-in) round sandwich tins
2 20-cm (8-in) round sandwich tins
12-hole bun (patty) tray
17.5 x 27.5-cm (7 x 11-in) Swiss roll (jelly roll) tin
22.5 x 32.5-cm (9 x 13-in) Swiss roll tin
20-cm (8-in) square deep cake tin
22.5-cm (9-in) ring tin

Lining cake tins (pans)

Most cake tins (pans) have to be prepared before baking to prevent the mixture sticking to the metal as the cake cooks. To prepare a tin, it should be greased with melted margarine or oil, then a little flour should be shaken around the tin and discarded. Alternatively, the tin can be greased and lined with greased greaseproof or non-stick paper, especially when baking a rich fruit or sponge cake. Follow the manufacturer's instructions for preparation if you are using non-stick tins.

Base-lining a tin (pan)

Use this method for most light cake mixtures, such as Victoria sandwiches, whisked sponges and light fruit cakes.

Place the base of the tin (pan) on a single sheet of greaseproof or non-stick paper. Draw around the outline of the base with a pencil. Cut around the outline with a pair of scissors. Grease the base and sides of the tin. Place the paper in the base and grease it.

Double-lining a deep cake tin (pan)

Rich fruit cakes, which require long cooking times, need to be protected during baking with greased double-thickness greaseproof or non-stick paper. Tying a double thickness strip of brown paper around the outside of the tin (pan), and placing another between the cake tin and baking tray, also helps to insulate the cake and stop it over-browning.

Cut a strip of double-thickness greaseproof or non-stick paper long enough to wrap around the outside of the tin with a small overlap. Fold the bottom edge up 2cm (¾in) and crease it firmly. The paper should be wide enough to stand 2.5cm (1in) above the top of the tin. Open out the folded edge and make slanting cuts at 2.5-cm (1-in) intervals all around. Place the tin on a double thickness of greaseproof paper and draw around the base.

With a pair of scissors, cut out the shape, keeping just inside the marked line. Grease the base and sides of the tin. Place one piece of paper in the base of the tin and grease lightly. Place the long strip in the tin, pressing it onto the sides with the cut edges spread over the base. Grease the side paper lightly. Place the second sheet of paper in the base of the tin, over the cut edges of the side sheets, and grease again.

Lining a shallow oblong tin (pan)

Lining the base and sides of a Swiss roll (jelly roll) tin makes it easier to remove the cooked cake.

Cut out a piece of greaseproof or non-stick paper about 7.5cm (3in) larger than the size of the tin (pan). Place the tin on the paper and draw around the base with a pencil. Make cuts from each corner to the marked edge. Grease the tin and press the paper onto the base. Press it neatly into the corners, overlapping the cuts in the paper. Grease the paper.

Using purchased cakes

When time is short, using a bought cake is often the only answer. Your local baker may even make the cake to the required size, ready to be decorated. Swiss (jelly) rolls are particularly useful for making cakes in such shapes as trains, rockets and chocolate logs. Use mini rolls to form the wheels and chimneys. Slab cakes are easy to cut into special shapes, such as cars, horses or boats. Use round jam biscuits for the wheels and mints with holes in the centre for the lifebelts. To make a treasure chest, slice off the top of a slab cake and hollow out the inside, then ice the outside and fill with sweets and chocolate coins.

A round sandwich cake provides the base for many of the cakes in this book. Choose a firm sponge that will be able to take the icing and decorations. If the cake is particularly crumbly, brush it with warmed sieved apricot jam before you ice it.

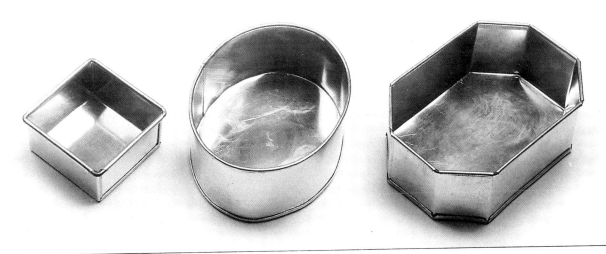

SPONGE CAKE RECIPES

Victoria sandwich cake

This universally popular cake can be baked in various shapes to form the base for novelty cakes. The all-in-one method saves both time and energy and is virtually foolproof. Use block margarine at room temperature or soft tub margarine straight from the fridge. If you are planning to cut the cake into shapes, it is best to make it the previous day to allow it to become firm. This recipe is worked out on a ratio of one egg to 50g (2oz) each of fat, sugar and flour, so you can increase or decrease the quantities given below according to the size of the cake you wish to cook.

Ingredients
175g (6oz) soft margarine
175g (6oz) caster (superfine) sugar
3 eggs, lightly beaten
175g (6oz) self-raising flour, sifted
7.5ml (1½ tsp) baking powder

Equipment
**2 x 20-cm (8-in) lined and greased round
sandwich tins (pans)
mixing bowl
wooden spoon
metal beater or electric mixer
wire cooling rack**

Heat the oven to 160°C (325°F) Gas Mark 3. Place all the cake ingredients in the bowl and mix well with the wooden spoon, then beat with the metal beater for 2-3 minutes until the mixture is light and fluffy. Using the electric mixer should take between 1-2 minutes. Divide the mixture between the cake tins and smooth the tops. Bake for 30-35 minutes or until the cakes are golden brown and springy to the touch. Leave the cakes to cool for 5 minutes, then turn out onto the wire cooling rack and remove the greaseproof paper. Leave until cold before filling and icing.

Variations
Chocolate Blend 30ml (2 tbsp) cocoa with 30ml (2 tbsp) boiling water until smooth. Add to the cake ingredients and mix well.
Coffee Dissolve 10ml (2 tsp) instant coffee in 15ml (1 tbsp) hot water and add to the cake ingredients. Alternatively, you can add 10ml (2 tsp) coffee essence.
Lemon or orange Add 10ml (2 tsp) finely-grated orange or lemon rind to the cake ingredients and mix well.

Quantities
The amount of cake mixture given above is enough to fill the following tin (pan) sizes:

**1 22.5-cm (9-in) round sandwich tin
1 17.5 x 27.5-cm (7 x 11-in) Swiss roll (jelly roll) tin
1 20-cm (8-in) round cake tin
1 17.5-20-cm (7-8-in) square cake tin
1 1.2-litre (2-pint) pudding basin
26 paper cake cases or individual bun (patty) tins**

Madeira cake

This firm sponge cake makes a good base for decorating. It is an alternative to fruit cake mixtures, and can be used for a sponge layer in a wedding cake. The mixture will make a 17.5-cm (7-in) round cake or a 15-cm (6-in) square cake.

Ingredients
**100g (4oz) butter
100g (4oz) sugar
2 medium-sized eggs
100g (4oz) self-raising flour, sifted
25g (1oz) plain (all-purpose) flour, sifted
50g (2oz) ground almonds
juice of medium-sized lemon**

Equipment
**17.5-cm (7-in) round or 15-cm (6-in)
square cake tin (pan), greased and lined
mixing bowl
wooden spoon or electric mixer
sieve
lemon squeezer
wire cooling rack**

Cream the butter and sugar together until light and fluffy. Beat the eggs and gradually beat into the creamed mixture. Sift together the flours and ground almonds, then fold into the creamed mixture together with the lemon juice. Pour into a greased baking tin and bake at 160°C (325°F) Gas Mark 3 for 40 minutes or until risen and golden brown on top and springy to the touch. Turn out onto a wire cooling rack, remove the lining paper and leave until cold.

Whisked sponge cake

This cake is light, airy and perfect for fresh cream cakes and other light confections. As the eggs and the sugar need to be whisked for several minutes, which can be tiring, a hand-held electric whisk is very useful. An electric mixer can also be used if you warm and thoroughly dry the bowl before beginning to whisk the mixture.

Ingredients
2 eggs
50g (2oz) caster (superfine) sugar
50g (2oz) plain (all-purpose) flour, sifted
2.5ml (½ tsp) baking powder
jam, buttercream or whipped cream and/or fruit

Equipment
2 17.5-cm (7-in) greased and lined round sandwich tins (pans)
mixing bowl
saucepan of hot water
hand-held electric whisk or electric mixer
large metal spoon
spatula
wire cooling rack

Heat the oven to 180°C (350°F) Gas Mark 4. Place the eggs and sugar in the mixing bowl and set over the saucepan of hot, but not boiling, water. Whisk until the mixture is thick and pale, and leaves a trail on the surface when the whisk is lifted up. This will take 5-10 minutes. Remove from the heat and whisk for a further 2 minutes. Shake the sifted flour and baking powder onto the surface of the mixture and fold in carefully with a large metal spoon or the whisk. Divide the mixture between the two lined and greased tins, then shake the tins lightly to get the surfaces level. Bake for 20-25 minutes until lightly browned and springy to the touch. Loosen the edges of the cakes with your fingertips or a spatula, then turn them out onto a cooling rack and remove the lining paper. Leave until cold before sandwiching the cakes together with jam, buttercream, whipped cream and/or fruit.

Variations
Chocolate Replace 15g (½oz) of plain flour with the same quantity of sifted cocoa powder.
Coffee Add 10ml (2 tsp) of coffee essence at the same time as the flour.
Lemon or orange Add 5ml (1 tsp) of finely-grated lemon or orange rind at the same time as the flour.

Swiss roll (jelly roll)

Ingredients
3 eggs
75g (3oz) caster (superfine) sugar
75g (3oz) plain (all-purpose) flour, sifted
2.5ml (½ tsp) baking powder
caster (superfine) sugar, for sprinkling
90ml (6 tbsp) warmed jam

Equipment
22.5 x 32.5-cm (9 x 13-in) greased and lined Swiss roll (jelly roll) tin
mixing bowl
saucepan of hot water
hand-held electric whisk or electric mixer
large metal spoon
palette knife
sheet of greaseproof paper
sharp knife

Heat the oven to 180°C (350°F) Gas Mark 4. Place the eggs and sugar in the mixing bowl and set over the saucepan of hot, but not boiling, water. Whisk until the mixture is thick and pale, and leaves a trail on the surface when the whisk is lifted up. This will take 5-10 minutes. Remove from the heat and whisk for a further 2 minutes. Shake the sifted flour and baking powder on to the surface of the mixture and fold in carefully with a large metal spoon or the whisk. Pour the mixture into the prepared tin (pan) and shake lightly to get the surface level. Bake for 10-12 minutes, or until lightly browned and springy to the touch, then leave to cool in the tin for 5 minutes. Cut out a piece of greaseproof paper slightly larger than the cake tin, place on the clean working surface and sprinkle it evenly with caster sugar. Turn the cake out onto the paper and remove the lining paper. Trim off any crusty edges with the sharp knife, then spread the jam evenly over the cake and roll up from one of the shorter ends, using the sugared paper to help you. When the cake is rolled up, leave until cold. If you intend to fill the Swiss roll (jelly roll) with whipped cream or buttercream, roll it up unfilled with a sheet of greaseproof paper inside it until cool, then carefully unroll and fill it.

FRUIT CAKE RECIPES

Rich fruit cake

Make this rich fruit cake for weddings, christenings and any other special occasions. You can bake it several months in advance because it improves with keeping. To store the cake, wrap it first in a double thickness of greaseproof paper, then in a layer of aluminium foil. Sprinkle the underside of the cake with 15ml (1 tbsp) brandy or sherry every couple of weeks to keep it moist and enrich its taste. Store the cake in a cool, dry place.

When making a large cake, you may find that your mixing bowl is not big enough for all the ingredients. Use a preserving pan or a clean plastic washing-up bowl instead.

Packaged dried fruit is usually pre-washed when you buy it, but it is always a good idea to check for any stray stalks. Loose dried fruit should be rinsed in cold water and dried thoroughly before use. Spread it out on trays lined with kitchen paper and leave to dry in a warm place overnight before using. Rinse and dry glacé cherries before using them to remove any excess sugar.

Rich Fruit Cake Ingredients

Round	15cm (6in)	17.5cm (7in)	20cm (8in)	22.5cm (9in)	25cm (10in)	27.5cm (11in)	30cm (12in)	
Square	12.5cm (5in)	15cm (6in)	17.5cm (7in)	20cm (8in)	22.5cm (9in)	25cm (10in)	27.5cm (11in)	30cm (12in)
currants	150g (5oz)	225g (8oz)	350g (12oz)	450g (1lb)	625g (1lb 6oz)	800g (1lb 12oz)	1.1kg (2½lb)	1.4kg (3lb)
sultanas	50g (2oz)	90g (3½oz)	140g (4½oz)	200g (7oz)	225g (8oz)	375g (13oz)	400g (14oz)	500g (1lb 2oz)
raisins	50g (2oz)	90g (3½oz)	140g (4½oz)	200g (7oz)	225g (8oz)	375g (13oz)	400g (14oz)	500g (1lb 2oz)
glacé cherries	40g (1½oz)	65g (2½oz)	75g (3oz)	125g (4oz)	150g (5oz)	225g (8oz)	325g (11oz)	350g (12oz)
cut mixed peel	25g (1oz)	50g (2oz)	50g (2oz)	75g (3oz)	125g (4oz)	150g (5oz)	200g (7oz)	250g (9oz)
blanched almonds	25g (1oz)	50g (2oz)	50g (2oz)	75g (3oz)	125g (4oz)	150g (5oz)	200g (7oz)	250g (9oz)
lemons	¼	½	¾	1	1	1	1½	2
plain (all-purpose) flour	90g (3½oz)	175g (6oz)	215g (7½oz)	350g (12oz)	400g (14oz)	600g (1lb 5oz)	700g (1½lb)	825g (1lb 13oz)
ground cinnamon	2.5ml (¼ tsp)	2.5ml (¼ tsp)	4ml (¾ tsp)	5ml (1 tsp)	7.5ml (1¼ tsp)	10ml (2 tsp)	12.5ml (2¼ tsp)	14ml (2¾ tsp)
ground nutmeg	1ml (¼ tsp)	1ml (¼ tsp)	2.5ml (½ tsp)	2.5ml (½ tsp)	4ml (¾ tsp)	5ml (1 tsp)	6ml (1¼ tsp)	7.5ml (1½ tsp)
ground mixed spice	1ml (¼ tsp)	1ml (¼ tsp)	2.5ml (½ tsp)	2.5ml (½ tsp)	4ml (¾ tsp)	5ml (1 tsp)	6ml (1¼ tsp)	7.5ml (1¼ tsp)
butter	75g (3oz)	150g (5oz)	175g (6oz)	300g (10oz)	350g (12oz)	500g (1lb 2oz)	600g (1lb 5oz)	800g (1lb 12oz)
soft dark brown sugar	75g (3oz)	150g (5oz)	175g (6oz)	300g (10oz)	350g (12oz)	500g (1lb 2oz)	600g (1lb 5oz)	800g (1lb 12oz)
large eggs	1½	2½	3	5	6	9	11	14
cooking time (approx)	2 hours	2½ hours	2¾ hours	3¼ hours	3¾ hours	4¼ hours	5¼ hours	6 hours
brandy or sherry (optional)	30ml (2 tbsp)	45ml (3 tbsp)	45ml (3 tbsp)	60ml (4 tbsp)	75ml (5 tbsp)	90ml (6 tbsp)	105ml (7 tbsp)	120ml (8 tbsp)

Ingredients
See chart.

Equipment
**1 cake tin (pan) of appropriate size,
greased and lined
mixing bowls
sharp knife
lemon grater
wooden spoon
sieve
electric mixer
large metal spoon
double thickness of brown paper
string
fine skewer
wire cooling rack**

Heat the oven to 150°C (300°F) Gas Mark 2. Mix together the currants, sultanas, raisins and mixed peel. Quarter the glacé cherries and add to the dried fruit. Chop the almonds, finely grate the lemon rind and add to the fruit, stirring them together well. Sift the flour and spices and put to one side in a separate bowl. Beat the butter and sugar together until light and fluffy – this should take about 10 minutes, or 5 minutes with a mixer. Lightly beat the eggs, then add to the creamed mixture a little at a time, also adding some sifted flour to prevent the mixture curdling. Fold in the remaining flour and mix well, then fold in the dried fruit, stirring until all the ingredients are thoroughly mixed. Turn the mixture into the prepared tin (pan), pressing it down well and smoothing the top with the back of a metal spoon. Tie a double thickness of brown paper around the outside of the tin. Bake the cake for the specified cooking time (see chart), checking the cake 30 minutes before the cake is due to be removed from the oven. To test if the cake is done, insert a fine skewer into the centre – if it comes out clean, the cake is cooked. Leave the cake in the tin to cool, then turn out, remove the paper and leave until cool on the wire rack. Prick the base of the cake at intervals with the skewer and spoon over the brandy or sherry. Allow to soak in, then wrap the cake and store for up to three months.

Crystallized fruit cake

This cake is much lighter than the traditional rich fruit cake. It can be covered with marzipan and icing to make an unusual but delicious cake for Christmas or a special occasion. Alternatively, arrange rows of nuts and glacé fruits over the top after baking it.

Ingredients
**50g (2oz) glacé cherries
50g (2oz) blanched almonds
50g (2oz) glacé pineapple, chopped
50g (2oz) crystallized ginger, chopped
50g (2oz) glacé peaches or pears, chopped
250g (8oz) butter
250g (8oz) caster (superfine) sugar
4 eggs, lightly beaten
125g (4oz) ground almonds
few drops almond essence
250g (8oz) plain (all-purpose) flour, sifted
5ml (1 tsp) baking powder**

Equipment
**1 20-cm (8-in) greased and lined round
cake tin (pan)
mixing bowl
sharp knife
wooden spoon or electric mixer
sieve
metal spoon
fine skewer
wire cooling rack**

Heat the oven to 140°C (275°F) Gas Mark 1. Rinse and dry the glacé cherries, then cut into quarters. Roughly chop the almonds, then mix together the cherries, almonds, pineapple, ginger, and peaches or pears. Cream together the butter and sugar until light and fluffy – this should take about 10 minutes, or 5 minutes if using an electric mixer. Beat in the eggs, a little at a time, beating well after each addition. Stir in the ground almonds, almond essence and mixed fruits, and mix well. Fold in the sifted flour and baking powder and stir carefully until evenly mixed. Press the mixture into the prepared tin, smoothing the top with the back of a metal spoon. Bake for 3-3½ hours. To test that the cake is cooked, insert a fine skewer into the centre. If it comes out clean, the cake is done. Remove from the oven and leave the cake to cool in the tin, then turn out, remove the lining paper and leave on the wire rack until cold.

SIMPLE ICINGS

Here are recipes for four easy icings. Their flavours can be varied following the instructions here or using your own imagination. For instance, you could decorate a chocolate cake with green-coloured icing flavoured with peppermint essence for a minty taste.

Glacé icing

Use this glossy water icing to coat cakes, both large and small, and biscuits.

This quantity will cover the top of a 20-cm (8-in) cake.

Ingredients
225g (8oz) icing (confectioner's) sugar, sifted
30-45ml (2-3 tbsp) boiling water
liquid edible food colouring if necessary

Equipment
mixing bowl
wooden spoon or electric mixer

Sift the icing (confectioner's) sugar into the mixing bowl and gradually beat in enough water to give a smooth shiny icing that will coat the back of a spoon. Beat in a few drops of edible food colouring if desired. Use the icing at once, or cover tightly with cling film until needed.

Sugarpaste

This icing is perfect for beginners. It is simple to make and can be rolled out like pastry to cover a Victoria sandwich or rich fruit cake. Unlike royal icing, it stays fairly soft on the cake, making cutting much easier and maybe suiting some people's teeth better, too! Once you have coloured it, you can use it to make moulded shapes, such as animals and flowers. Liquid glucose is available from chemists.

This quantity will cover the top and sides of a 20-cm (8-in) round cake.

Ingredients
450g (1lb) icing (confectioner's) sugar, sifted
1 egg white, lightly beaten
15ml (1 rounded tbsp) liquid glucose
sifted icing (confectioner's) sugar for kneading

Equipment
mixing bowl
wooden spoon or electric mixer
rolling pin

Sift the icing (confectioner's) sugar into a mixing bowl. Add the egg white and glucose and mix together until the ingredients start to cling together, then knead well with your fingers to form a soft mixture. Turn out onto a clean flat surface lightly sprinkled with sifted icing sugar and continue kneading until the icing is smooth, silky and pliable – this should take about 5 minutes. Roll out the icing and use immediately, or wrap in cling film and store in a tightly-sealed polythene bag in the fridge until needed.

Buttercream

Ideal for covering and filling sponges, sandwich and madeira cakes, buttercream is a very versatile icing that's also extremely simple to make. You can smooth it with a palette knife to give a flat finish, swirl it into patterns with the tines of a fork or pull it into peaks with the tip of a knife. Colour and flavour it to match the cake mixture, or to give added interest to a plain sponge.

This quantity will fill and cover the top of a 17.5-cm (7-in) sandwich cake.

Ingredients
125g (4oz) unsalted or slightly salted butter, softened
225g (8oz) icing (confectioner's) sugar, sifted
15ml (1 tbsp) fruit juice or milk

Equipment
mixing bowl
wooden spoon or electric mixer

Place the softened butter, sifted icing (confectioner's) sugar and liquid in a bowl and mix until all the ingredients have blended together. Beat the icing well for 2-3 minutes until it is light and fluffy. Transfer to a covered container and store for up to one week in the fridge. Bring to room temperature before using.

Variations

Chocolate Blend 15ml (1 tbsp) cocoa with 15ml (1 tbsp) hot water to give a smooth paste. Beat into the icing.

Coffee Replace the liquid with the same amount of coffee essence or 5ml (1 tsp) instant coffee dissolved in 10ml (2 tsp) hot water.

Orange or lemon Replace the liquid with the same amount of lemon or orange juice and add 5ml (1 tsp) finely-grated lemon or orange rind. You can use a few drops of edible food colouring to deepen the colour of the icing if you wish.

Vanilla Add 2.5ml (½ tsp) vanilla essence to the icing mixture.

Royal icing

Royal icing is used mainly to decorate rich fruit and Christmas cakes which have first been covered with a layer of marzipan. When making royal icing for a tiered wedding cake, make batches of up to 900g (2lb) and store them in sealed plastic containers until ready for use. If you make the icing with an electric mixer, cover the bowl with a clean damp cloth and leave for 3-4 hours to allow any air bubbles to disperse. Glycerine can be added to keep the icing soft. The icing can be smoothed to give a flat surface, or pulled into peaks with a knife for a rough frosted effect.

This quantity will cover the top and sides of a 25-cm (10-in) square cake.

Ingredients
2 egg whites
450g (1lb) icing (confectioner's) sugar, sifted
5ml (1 tsp) lemon juice
5ml (1 tsp) glycerine, if desired

Equipment
mixing bowl
metal whisk or electric mixer
wooden spoon

Place the egg whites in a clean mixing bowl and beat lightly until just beginning to froth. Gradually beat in half the icing (confectioner's) sugar with a wooden spoon. Add the lemon juice and glycerine, if you are using it, and half the remaining icing sugar. Beat until smooth and very white. Gradually beat in enough icing sugar to give you the consistency you want. The icing should form soft peaks if you are coating a cake, but it should be much stiffer for piping.

Piping techniques

As with most skills, practice makes perfect, so don't despair if you find it difficult to pipe properly at first. Royal icing is the most difficult medium to use, as the icing quickly hardens and it's not easy to correct mistakes. Begin with a nylon piping bag fitted with a large savoy tube and practice piping mashed potato. This can be re-used several times. Once you have experimented with the various nozzle shapes you'll soon build up confidence and be ready to move on from potato to real icing.

Practice with buttercream next, again using large nozzles. When choosing a piping bag, try to find a large one with a screw adaptor, because this will convert the bag for use with small nozzles. These can be changed without replacing the bag. The buttercream should be fairly soft when piping, so add a few drops of hot water if it is too stiff. You should be able to pull the buttercream into softish peaks so that it can be used to work designs of shells, stars and rosettes on a cake. However, it is not suitable for fine writing work.

Glacé icing can be used to pipe lines, lacework and writing, but it must be of a stiffer consistency than that used to coat a cake. Beat in more sifted icing (confectioner's) sugar until it reaches the desired thickness.

The consistency of royal icing is determined by the type of piping you are planning. It should stand in well-formed but not hard peaks when piping dots, shells, stars and rosettes, but should be a little softer for writing or piping lines, or the icing will break.

If you are unsure of your design or of the consistency of the icing, practice piping on an up-turned tin until you feel confident enough to pipe directly onto the cake. Flat iced cakes should be left to dry for 24 hours before they are decorated.

Making shapes

Marzipan and moulding icing are both excellent for making moulded or cut-out cake decorations. Moulding icing is slightly easier to colour than marzipan, as it is white. However, white marzipan is now commonly available and gives equally good results.

One very effective way of decorating a cake is to make animal shapes. If making a cake for a child, choose their favourite animals, and give them hats, clothes or funny faces. Try making elephants, cats, mice or Easter chicks, or for Christmas make a snowman with a hat and scarf to decorate the cake. You could make a few snowballs to complete the scene. Flowers are simple to mould and can be built up petal by petal, or try making a selection of fruits to decorate an Easter or Mother's Day cake.

Cut-out decorations are simpler still, particularly if you have some fancy cutters in the shapes of such things as leaves, stars, trees and moons. To decorate a Christmas cake, cut out green-coloured marzipan holly leaves and add a few red marzipan berries for good measure.

To colour marzipan or moulding icing, place the amount you wish to colour on a plate. Using a cocktail stick, add the edible food colouring, a drop at a time, and knead it in thoroughly until the mixture is evenly coloured and no longer streaky. Add extra sifted icing (confectioner's) sugar if the icing or marzipan becomes too sticky. To make dark colours, concentrated colourings give the quickest results. Add a touch of brown colouring or gravy browning if the colour is too bright. Allow the decorations to dry by placing them in empty egg boxes or wire cooling racks.

BASIC PIPING

Piping straight lines

Place the tip of the writing nozzle at the place where the icing is to begin. Press the icing out of the bag slowly, then lift the nozzle about 2.5cm (1in) above the cake. Move your hand steadily in the direction of the line to be piped, keeping the icing flowing evenly. At about 1cm (½in) before the end of the line, stop squeezing the bag and lower the nozzle gently onto the cake. Break off the icing by lifting the bag.

Piping dots and stars

Use a writing nozzle to make dots, and a star nozzle to make the stars. Insert the correct nozzle in the piping bag, then hold the bag upright so that the nozzle just touches the cake. Squeeze the bag gently, at the same time lifting the nozzle to allow the icing to flow out. Stop squeezing when the dot or star is the correct size, then quickly remove the nozzle. If you wish to pipe coloured dots onto the cake, it is best to overpipe them onto a row of white dots, to avoid the colour leaking into the flat icing. Let the dots dry before overpiping them.

Piping trellis work

This is a very popular way of using straight lines. Fit a writing tube into the piping bag, then pipe a series of parallel straight lines in one direction and leave to dry. Now pipe a second row of lines at right angles to the first and leave to dry. You can add a further two or three rows of lines to give a three-dimensional effect, allowing each set to dry between applications. If you make a mistake when piping, the wet line of icing can be removed from the cake with a fine skewer.

Piping curved lines and writing

Scrolls, loops and writing are all techniques that require practice, but they can be easily worked once you have mastered control of the icing. Draw your design, or write the words, onto a sheet of greaseproof paper, then place this in position on the iced surface of the cake and carefully transfer the design by pricking through the paper to the icing with a pin. Remove the greaseproof paper, then pipe the design, following the pinpricks, with white icing. Allow this to dry, then overpipe with coloured icing if desired.

Scribbling or cornelli work

This is a very simple but effective decoration. The finished design looks like lace, and it can be piped onto the top or sides of a cake. Insert a fine or medium writing nozzle in the piping bag. Hold the nozzle almost upright and just above the surface of the cake, then move the nozzle around to make a swirling pattern.

Making and filling a paper piping bag

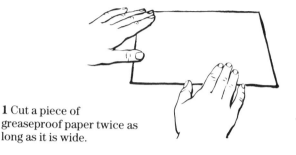

1 Cut a piece of greaseproof paper twice as long as it is wide.

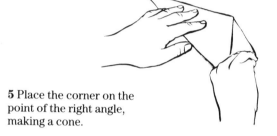

5 Place the corner on the point of the right angle, making a cone.

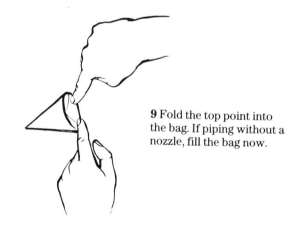

9 Fold the top point into the bag. If piping without a nozzle, fill the bag now.

12 Hold the top of the bag down and gently pull out the palette knife.

14

2 Fold the paper diagonally. The points will not meet.

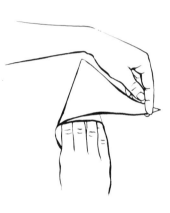

3 Cut along the fold with a sharp knife to make two right-angle triangles.

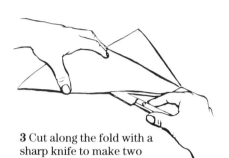

4 Lay one triangle flat with the right angle facing you, and fold the corner inwards.

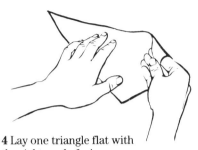

7 Wrap the corner around the cone twice so that the points meet.

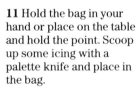

8 Slide the three points together to tighten the bag.

6 Put your fingers in the cone to hold it and bring the other corner over it.

11 Hold the bag in your hand or place on the table and hold the point. Scoop up some icing with a palette knife and place in the bag.

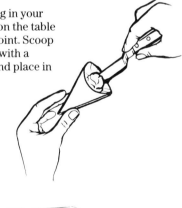

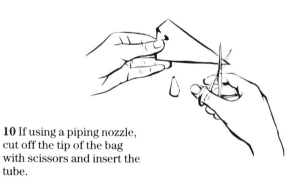

10 If using a piping nozzle, cut off the tip of the bag with scissors and insert the tube.

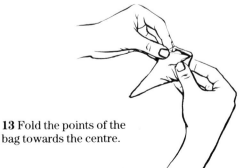

13 Fold the points of the bag towards the centre.

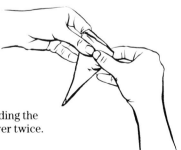

14 Fasten by folding the top of the bag over twice.

WORKING WITH MARZIPAN

Made into a paste from ground almonds, marzipan is an ideal way to cover a rich fruit or firm sponge cake before it is decorated with royal icing or sugarpaste. It prevents any stray cake crumbs mixing with the icing.

There are two ways of marzipanning a cake. If using royal icing, cut one piece of marzipan to cover the top of the cake and another for the sides, then mould the joins together. Sugarpaste and moulding icing, however, demand a much smoother base, so you must cover the top and sides of your cake with one large sheet of marzipan to enable the sugarpaste or icing to lie completely flat on the cake. When working with marzipan it is essential that it doesn't come into contact with flour or it will ferment.

Quantities
450-700g (1-1½lb) marzipan or sugarpaste covers a 15-cm (6-in) square or 17.5-cm (7-in) round cake
700-900g (1½-2lb) marzipan or sugarpaste covers a 20-cm (8-in) square or 22.5-cm (9-in) round cake
1.1-1.4kg (2½-3lb) marzipan or sugarpaste covers a 25-cm (10-in) square or 27.5-cm (11-in) round cake
1.8kg (4lb) marzipan or sugarpaste covers a 30-cm (12-in) square or 32.5-cm (13-in) round cake

Marzipanning a cake to use with royal icing

Place slightly less than half the marzipan on a clean flat surface lightly sprinkled with sifted icing (confectioner's) sugar, then roll it out until it is 2.5cm (1in) larger than the top of the cake. If it is very uneven, trim the top of the cake to give a flat surface. Brush the top of the cake with warmed sieved apricot jam, then invert the cake onto the marzipan. Using a small palette knife, draw up the edge of the marzipan, attaching it to the sides of the cake and making the top of the cake flat. Turn the cake right side up on a cake board. Cut two pieces of string, one the height of the cake and the other its circumference. Brush the sides of the cake with apricot jam. Roll out the remaining marzipan to a strip long enough and wide enough to fit around the cake, using the string as a guide. Loosely roll up the marzipan strip, then unroll it carefully onto the sides of the cake, pressing it on as you work. For large cakes, cover the sides with two shorter strips, which will be easier to handle. Smooth the joins in the marzipan with a small knife, then trim off the excess marzipan. Leave the cake uncovered in a dry place for at least 48 hours before icing.

Marzipanning a cake for royal icing

1 Roll out the marzipan evenly. Brush the bottom of the cake with warmed sieved apricot jam and quickly turn over onto the marzipan. Cut round with a sharp knife.

2 Measure the circumference of the cake with a piece of string.

3 Brush the sides of the cake with warmed sieved apricot jam.

4 Roll out a long strip of marzipan and cut it a little shorter than the circumference. Roll up the marzipan and unroll around the cake. Press in place with a jar or tin.

5 Use a sharp knife to trim off the excess marzipan.

6 Place the board on top of the marzipanned cake and turn over.

Marzipanning a cake to use with sugarpaste

Place the marzipan on a clean flat surface lightly dusted with sifted icing (confectioner's) sugar and knead until soft and smooth. Roll out a thin sausage of marzipan, fix it around the top edge of the cake with a little egg white or warmed sieved apricot jam and press into place with the knife. Now turn the cake over so that its flat bottom becomes the top. Fill any holes in the surface of the cake with small pieces of marzipan. Measure the cake up one side, across the top and down the other side, then roll out the marzipan until it is slightly larger than this measurement and between 6-12mm (¼-½in) thick. Paint the surface of the cake with the egg white or jam, then lift the marzipan, with the help of the rolling pin, onto the cake and smooth down the top to remove any air bubbles. If the cake is square, you must work on the four corners first. Flare out the marzipan from one corner to get rid of any pleats and, using the palm of your hand, ease the marzipan into the corner with an upward movement. If you drag your hand downwards, you could tear the marzipan around the top edge. Repeat at the other corners and then smooth down the sides. Use the same flaring technique and hand movements if the cake is round. Now run a marzipan smoother firmly over the surface of the cake. If any cracks or breaks form, repair them by vigorously rubbing your hands over the fissure. Trim the bottom edge of the cake with a knife to remove any excess marzipan, then rub the smoother over any rough edges to give a flat surface. Leave the cake for at least 48 hours in a dry place before icing.

Marzipanning a cake for sugarpaste

1 The cake is covered upside down from the way it was baked – the base will be the top of the finished cake. Peel off the lining paper and fill in any holes in the sides or top with small pieces of marzipan. Smooth over to get a level surface.

2 Turn the cake upside down. Brush the top and sides of the cake with warmed sieved apricot jam.

3 Dust the work surface with icing (confectioner's) sugar, never flour or cornflour. Roll out the marzipan with a rolling pin. Prevent it from sticking by lifting and rotating it, but do not turn it over.

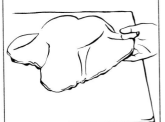

4 Carefully pick up the marzipan by draping it over the rolling pin.

5 Carefully drop the marzipan over the cake, lifting the edges slightly to help it fall without breaking.

6 Then cuddle in with the palms of your hands. Push up, don't pull down or the marzipan may tear. If the cake has corners, shape at the corners first. Flare out from the first corner to unfold any pleats, then ease the marzipan into the corner with an upward movement of the hand.

7 Use the palms of your hands carefully to smooth over the top of the cake. Repair any tears by rubbing over them with the heel of your hand in a circular motion.

8 Cut off the surplus marzipan level with the bottom of the cake, using a sharp knife.
  Use a smoother to push the cake to the edge of the surface. Lift by placing one hand under the cake and drop onto a prepared cake board. The marzipan must skin for a day or two before being covered with sugarpaste.

ICING THE CAKE

Covering a cake with royal icing

Royal icing gives a smooth or rough iced surface to a cake. To create rough icing, spread royal icing over the marzipanned cake surface with a palette knife and then pull into peaks with the blade of the knife. A smooth surface is created by applying several layers of royal icing. You will find this much easier if you use a cake turntable.

Quantities
450g (1lb) royal icing covers the top and sides of a 20-cm (8-in) cake

Position the marzipanned cake in the centre of a cake board, on a turntable if you have one, then place some royal icing, thick enough to stand in firm peaks in the mixing bowl, on the top of the cake. Using a straight-bladed or palette knife, spread the icing evenly over the cake surface using a paddling movement and rotating the cake. This eliminates any air bubbles. Hold the board with one hand and the knife with the other at a 45°

Covering a cake with royal icing

1 Place the marzipan-covered cake in the centre of a cake board, securing it with dabs of icing. Spread some royal icing over the top of the cake with a palette knife, using a paddling motion.

2 Holding a metal straight edge at 45° to the cake, smoothly draw the edge towards you and across the icing.

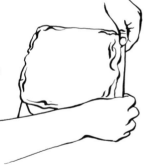

3 If the surface is not smooth enough, add more icing and smooth it again with the metal straight edge. Clean the edges of the icing by running a palette knife around the top of the cake, then leave to dry.

4 Spread icing over one side of the cake with a palette knife, using a paddling motion.

5 Smooth the icing down by drawing the metal straight edge or an icing comb over the surface. Ice the opposite side of the cake in the same way.

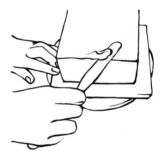

6 Remove any excess icing with the blade of the palette knife then leave to dry. Ice the other two sides of the cake the following day.

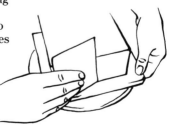

angle to the cake surface, and rotate the turntable to spread the icing evenly over the surface. Place the cake on a flat table and draw a metal straight edge across the top of the cake at a 45° angle, ensuring you don't press too hard. Place any surplus icing in the bowl, remove any icing from the sides of the cake and leave it to dry. Then place the cake on the turntable and spread icing down the sides of the cake, again using a palette knife in a paddling motion. Hold the cleaned straight edge at an angle to the cake sides, then steadily rotate the turntable until the sides of the cake are smooth. Gently remove the straight edge and clean any icing from the board. Leave to dry. Remove any rough icing edges once the cake is completely dry and the icing hard. The subsequent coats of icing should be slightly softer in consistency. A wedding cake should have three or four coats of icing, but you only need apply two coats for a less formal cake. If icing a square cake, ice alternate sides, allowing them to dry before working on the other two sides.

To ice the cake board, coat it with a thin layer of icing, then draw the straight edge across the icing, rotating the turntable at the same time. Clean the straight edge, then hold it at an angle of 45° to the wet icing and rotate the board again. Bevel the edges of the icing, clean any surplus icing from the sides of the board and leave to dry.

Covering a cake with sugarpaste

If using sugarpaste, you don't have to cover a cake with marzipan first. You can apply a thick layer of sugarpaste directly onto the surface of a cake, or you can use a thin layer of marzipan and a thin layer of sugarpaste to get a smoother surface.

Place the sugarpaste on a clean flat surface lightly sprinkled with sifted icing (confectioner's) sugar and knead until soft and pliable. Measure up one side of the cake, across the top and down the other side, then roll out the sugarpaste until it is slightly larger than this measurement. Using a clean cosmetic sponge, cover the surface of the cake with whisky, sherry or boiled water. This not only acts as a glue to make the sugarpaste stay in place but is also an antibacterial agent. Lift the sugarpaste onto the cake, with the help of the rolling pin, then smooth it into position, taking care not to tear it or trap any air bubbles. Smooth it over the top of the cake first, then work on the sides until it forms a flat covering. Prick any air bubbles with a pin, then rub over the surface of the sugarpaste to smooth it down. Rub a marzipan smoother over the surface of the sugarpaste to give the finishing touch. Trim around the base of the cake with a sharp knife to remove any excess or untidy edges.

The variety of ready-made decorations with which you can decorate cakes is almost endless, ranging from sweets to tiny toys. Once you have devised the theme for your cake, you will be able to think of many different ways of decorating it.

Sponge cakes can be decorated with all kinds of edible decorations to produce simple and effective birthday and novelty cakes. Sweets, mimosa balls, chocolate vermicelli, jelly shapes and sugar strands are just some of the shop-bought decorations that are extremely useful. If you're short of time, cover the top and sides of a cake with buttercream and press chocolate vermicelli or sugar strands onto the icing while it is still moist. Desiccated coconut can be tinted with edible food colouring and used to coat a cake spread with buttercream, or you can colour the coconut green and sprinkle it over a cake board brushed with honey to represent grass. To colour desiccated coconut, place it in a bowl, add a few drops of colouring and mix together until evenly tinted.

Chocolate coins, chocolate buttons and coloured sugar-coated chocolate sweets are all great favourites for cake decorating. Make a simple clock cake by placing chocolate buttons or coins around the cake and piping the numbers on top.

To decorate the top edge of a cake, overlap orange and lemon sugared slices, chocolate buttons, jelly sweets or halved chocolate mint wafers. Pipe whirls of buttercream around the cake and top with mimosa balls, slices of glacé cherries, nuts or crystallized fruits. A cluster of shop-bought marzipan fruits arranged in the centre of a cake gives instant colour, or try a posy.

Non-edible decorations can make a cake extra special and add that all-important personal touch. For a child's birthday, plan the cake around his or her hobby or special interest. Toy shops sell inexpensive figures of spacemen, farm animals, cowboys, soldiers and other characters suitable for cake decoration. For a farm cake, make a ploughed field from chocolate buttercream, combed with the tines of a fork, or grazing land from green glacé icing. Add shop-bought farm animals and a fence made from chocolate matchsticks. A lunar landscape is easily made from swirls of royal icing sprinkled with silver balls. Sugar flying saucers can be fixed around the edge of the cake, with spacemen dotted about to add the final touch. Easter eggs just need a few fluffy chicks, sugar eggs and a nest made from forked-up chocolate buttercream or crumbled flaked chocolate.

Card shops and large stationers sell an increasingly wide range of decorations for special occasions such as Christmas, Easter, weddings and engagements.

SIMPLE CAKE DESIGNS

Some of the simplest cake designs for children can also be the most effective, as you will see from the ideas given here. You can make any of the following cakes from a filled 20-cm (8-in) whisked sponge or all-in-one sandwich cake.

Flower cake
Spread the top of the cake with buttercream. Pipe the outline of the petals in contrasting buttercream and fill in the shapes with sugar flowers, jelly sweets or piped rosettes of buttercream. Fill the centre of the flower with contrasting coloured sweets.

Spider's web
Spread the top of the cake with white glacé icing. Pipe concentric rings of chocolate glacé icing quickly over the top, about 2.5cm (1in) apart. Immediately draw the point of a skewer from the centre to the outside edge of the rings, then continue around the cake to create a web. Fix a spider made from moulding icing or plastic to the top of the cake.

Face cakes
Spread the top of the cake with pink-tinted glacé icing or buttercream and create a face from sweets and cake decorations, using the following ideas as guidelines.

Hair Chocolate vermicelli, crumbled bars of flaked chocolate, coloured desiccated coconut or coconut strands.

Eyes Chocolate buttons, coloured sugar-coated chocolate sweets, jelly sweets.

Glasses Liquorice laces, cut and shaped.

Eyebrows Liquorice laces, crumbled bars of flaked chocolate or chocolate matchsticks.

Nose Glacé cherry, marshmallow, jelly sweet, orange or lemon slice cut to shape, jelly bean, liquorice comfit, silver dragée.

Cheeks Gold chocolate coins, glacé cherries, sugar flying saucers.

Mouth Liquorice laces (preferably red), row of jelly sweets, small square mints for teeth.

Ears Ice cream wafers cut to shape and fixed to the cake with little dabs of icing.

Earrings Candy shell sweets, coloured sugar-coated chocolate sweets, liquorice allsorts, silver dragées.

FRESH CREAM CAKE

Ingredients
22.5-cm (9-in) long rectangular sponge cake
800ml (1½ pints) double (heavy) cream
assortment of small jellied sweets in
different shapes and colours

Equipment
25-cm (10-in) square cake board
sharp knife
pastry brush
metal or electric whisk
metal spoon
large piping bag
No15 star nozzle
1m (1 yard) broiderie anglaise
1m (1 yard) red ribbon 6mm (¼in) wide

Using a sharp knife, cut the cake into the 1 shape, as shown in the diagram. Remove any loose crumbs with a pastry brush and place the cake on the board. Whip the cream until it is very thick and holds its shape when the whisk or beaters are removed. Spoon into the piping bag fitted with a No15 star nozzle and begin decorating the sides of the cake. Place the end of the piping tube flat on the board and next to the cake. Press and pull up straight against the side of the cake, then stop pressing and pull the tube directly away at the top. Work in this way until the sides of the cake are covered, with the lines of cream touching but not overlapping. You will need to refill the bag several times. When the sides are covered, pipe long lines of cream to cover the top of the cake. Start at the top of the 1, place the tube against the cake and quickly pull it towards you in a straight line. When the top is covered, hide the seam between the top and sides by piping stars around the edge. Finish off by piping star rosettes, using the same nozzle, at intervals on the top of the cake and decorate with jellied sweets. Thread the red ribbon through the broiderie anglaise, then arrange it around the sides of the board.

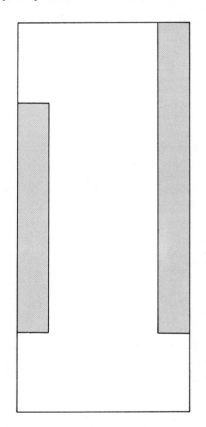

Decorating with fresh cream

Fresh cream can be used to fill, coat and decorate sponge cakes. Use double (heavy) cream, which whips quickly and holds its shape well. To whip cream, pour it into a large, clean bowl and whisk continuously, using a hand-held electric mixer, egg-beater or wire whisk. If the cream is for coating or piping it should stand in soft peaks and hold its shape when the whisk or beaters are removed. Do not over-beat, or the cream will become thick and lumpy.

You can colour or flavour the cream if you wish. To do this, whisk until it starts to thicken, then add a small amount of sifted icing (confectioner's) sugar, flavouring extract or liquid food colouring. Continue whisking until the cream forms soft peaks.

To coat cakes with fresh cream, spoon it onto the cake surface and spread it over the top and sides with a palette knife. It will not be possible to get a perfectly smooth surface but you can create a textured surface with an icing comb.

To pipe fresh cream, use large tubes and large piping bags made from double-thickness greaseproof paper. If doing a lot of piping, you will need to have several bags ready, or refill the same bag, rather than using one very large bag. This is because the heat from your hands softens the cream, making piping difficult after a while.

HUMPTY DUMPTY CAKE

Ingredients
3-egg sponge cake mixture
200g (7oz) marzipan
black, red, yellow, green and blue edible food colourings
350g (12oz) chocolate buttercream
150g (5oz) milk baker's (compound) chocolate or milk
chocolate buttons
melted chocolate

Equipment
900-g (2-lb) loaf tin (pan), greased and lined
25 x 20-cm (10 x 8-in) cake board
non-stick baking paper
wire cooling rack
mixing bowl
pan of hot water
palette knife
sharp knife
bowl of boiling water

Bake the sponge cake mixture in the greased and lined loaf tin (pan), then turn out onto a wire cooling rack and leave until cold. Wash the tin, then line it with a sheet of non-stick baking paper. Melt the baker's chocolate, if using it, in a bowl over a pan of hot water, or place for 2 minutes in a microwave oven. Beat until smooth, then pour it into the prepared tin and tip it until the chocolate forms an even layer on the bottom. Allow to set – this should take about 15 minutes in the fridge or 40 minutes at room temperature. When the chocolate is firm, gently lift the sheet of baking paper out of the tin and place on a clean flat surface. Heat the sharp knife by dipping the blade in a jug of boiling water, drying it and quickly cutting the chocolate into six long strips (see diagram). Next, cut these strips into brick shapes, carefully peel the chocolate rectangles away from the baking paper and place on a flat surface. Using a palette knife, cover the cake evenly with the chocolate buttercream, then arrange the chocolate pieces or chocolate buttons over the cake, pressing them in place fairly firmly and spacing them to look like bricks. Now place the cake on the board, securing it in place with dabs of buttercream or melted chocolate. To make the Humpty Dumpty figure, take 140g (5oz) of the marzipan, saving a small piece to make his arms, and roll it between your palms until it is egg-shaped. Colour the remaining marzipan as follows: 20g (¾oz) green, 20g (¾oz) yellow, 5g (¼oz) red, 5g (¼oz) blue and 5g (¼oz) black. Divide the last 5g (¼oz) and colour it to make Humpty Dumpty's features and the snail. Make four long sausages from the green marzipan, keeping a little to one side to make flower stems, then flatten and attach them to Humpty Dumpty's body to form the top of his trousers. They should stick naturally, but if not, fix them in place with dabs of melted chocolate. Make two long sausages from the uncoloured marzipan, reserving small pieces to form the flowers, until they look like legs, then attach them to Humpty Dumpty's body. Make his shoes from the black marzipan and attach them with melted chocolate. Now make two arms from the small piece of uncoloured marzipan and fix them to the body. With the blue marzipan, make the hat and put it on Humpty Dumpty's head, then give him a face – you can use sweets instead of marzipan if you wish. Roll out the remaining green marzipan to make the stems and leaves, fix them to the wall with melted chocolate, then make the flowers by forming small balls, flattening one side of them and making two cuts to represent petals. Position at the top of the stems and fix to the wall with melted chocolate. Make the snail and ladybird with the remaining pieces of marzipan.

Ingredients
20-cm (8-in) square sponge cake
made with 4 eggs
350g (12oz) yellow-coloured buttercream
350g (12oz) chocolate buttercream
350g (12oz) uncoloured buttercream
warmed sieved apricot jam
liquorice allsorts
bar of flaked chocolate
coloured sugar-coated chocolate sweets
chocolate matchsticks
small squares of fudge
melted chocolate
3 marzipan pigs

Equipment
large tray, cake board or
covered bread board
palette knife
sharp knife
fork

Cut the cake into four equal pieces, 5cm (2in) square. Three of the squares make the houses, and the fourth makes the roofs. Cut this square in half horizontally, then cut triangles from the middle of each slice to the lower outside edge. This will give you two large triangles and four small ones in all. Spread warmed sieved apricot jam over the tops of the three squares, then cover two of them with the large triangles, to make roofs. For the third, place two of the small triangles together to form a roof shape, and fix these to the top of the cake. Cut out a square in one side of the roof, cut one of the remaining triangles in half and join the two pieces together with jam to form a square, then fit this in the space left in the roof. This makes the chimney. To make the straw house, cover the top and sides with yellow buttercream, then mark it with the tines of the fork to resemble straw. Press liquorice sweets on the front for the windows and door. For the stick house, cover the cake with chocolate buttercream, then press coloured sweets in the front of the house to make the windows and door, vertical lines of chocolate matchsticks over the sides of the house, and a horizontal line of matchsticks to outline the edge of the roof. Cover the roof with crumbled bars of flaked chocolate. To make the brick house, spread the cake with uncoloured buttercream, then decorate with rows of coloured sugar-coated chocolate sweets and pieces of fudge for the windows.

Making marzipan pigs

Ingredients
250g (9oz) marzipan
yellow, red, blue and brown edible food colouring
melted chocolate

To make the pigs, put 25g (1oz) of the marzipan to one side, then colour the rest pink and divide it into three 75-g (3-oz) balls. Use 50g (2oz) to make each pig's body and 25g (1oz) to make the head, ears and limbs. For the body, roll the marzipan into a ball, for the head roll it into a cone shape and for the limbs roll it into two sausage shapes, then cut these in half horizontally. Use tiny pieces of the remaining marzipan to shape the ears, then assemble each pig, fixing them together with dabs of melted chocolate if necessary. Colour the rest of the marzipan to make the hats and features. Carefully arrange the houses and pigs on the large tray or cake board.

ANIMAL CRACKERS

Ingredients
20-cm (8-in) square sponge
made with 4 eggs
700g (1½lb) light green sugarpaste
450g (1lb) marzipan
warmed sieved apricot jam
yellow, green, brown and
black edible food colouring
melted chocolate
chocolate matchsticks

Equipment
30-cm (12-in) square cake board
sharp knife
brown ribbon
cocktail sticks (wooden toothpicks)

Spread the top and sides of the cake with warmed sieved apricot jam before covering it with the sugarpaste. Allow to dry for one day before decorating. Make the animals. Place the cake in the middle of the cake board, fixing it in place with dabs of melted chocolate, then arrange the chocolate matchsticks around the edge of the cake, holding them in position with dabs of melted chocolate. Tie one piece of ribbon along the top of the matchsticks, and another along the bottom, to make the fence. Carefully place the marzipan animals on top of the cake, if necessary securing them in place with hidden cocktail sticks (wooden toothpicks).

Making the panda
Use 40g (1½oz) uncoloured marzipan and roll into one ball for the body and one cone for the head, then attach the head to the body with melted chocolate. Colour 12g (½oz) marzipan black, keep a little to one side, then roll the rest into two sausages. Cut them in half horizontally to make two arms and two legs. Shape the ends to resemble paws, making nicks in them to form the claws. Attach to the body of the panda, then make five flattened circles. Flatten one side of two of them, then fix to the sides of the panda's head to make ears, and gently curve them. Fix two more circles to the head to make eyes, and use the final circle for the nose.

Making the elephant
Colour 75g (3oz) marzipan grey, then mould 12g (½oz) into the head, 50g (2oz) into the body and 15g (½oz) into the four legs. Join all the pieces together with dabs of melted chocolate, then allow to dry for a day before fixing the tusks in place, made from rolls of uncoloured marzipan.

Making the lion
Colour 40g (1½oz) of marzipan pale yellow and 12g (½oz) brown. Using the yellow, mould a ball for the body, a cone shape for the head and four thick sausages for the legs, then join them together with dabs of melted chocolate. Score lines at the ends of the legs to make paws. Roll out a sausage of brown marzipan to make the mane, then position at the back of the head and snip round with scissors to make the fur. Make another sausage of brown marzipan for the tail, attach to the back of the body and snip with the scissors. Make the eyes, nose and tuft of mane with more brown marzipan.

Making the kangaroo
Colour 75g (3oz) of marzipan brown. Make the head, body and tail in one piece, using most of the marzipan. Roll out sausages for the legs, and fix them in position with dabs of melted chocolate. Make the baby kangaroo, then attach it to the front of its mother with melted chocolate.

CHOCOLATE BOAT CAKE

Ingredients
22.5-cm (9-in) round sponge cake made
with 4 eggs
700g (1½lb) buttercream
various shades of edible food colouring,
including blue
175g (6oz) milk baker's (compound)
chocolate
10 chocolate matchsticks
300g (10oz) uncoloured marzipan

Equipment
30-cm (12-in) round plate or cake board
fork
10 paper cases or 5 dariole moulds
5 long strips of cardboard folded in half and
stapled
mixing bowl
pan of hot water
metal spoon

Colour the buttercream pale blue, then spread it over the top and sides of the cake. Pull into peaks with the tines of a fork, then place the cake on the plate or cake board. Put one paper case inside another, then fold them in the middle to make an oval shape. Fold the other cases in the same way, and place each pair of cases in the cardboard loops. This will give you five moulds. Put a little chocolate to one side, then melt the rest in a mixing bowl over a pan of hot water or place in a microwave oven for 2 minutes. Pour the chocolate into the moulds, using the back of the spoon to coat each mould properly to give a fairly thick layer. Leave to set, then gently peel off the cases and place on the buttercream sea.

Making the bears
Make the teddy bears from the uncoloured marzipan, leaving a little to one side for the features and hats. Make a cone for the head, a ball for the body and sausages for the arms and legs, then attach them together with dabs of the remaining melted chocolate. With brown marzipan make the eyes, noses, ears and paw pads, then mould the hats with different coloured pieces of marzipan. Place on the bears, gently sit them in their boats on the top of the cake and give them chocolate matchstick oars. If you wish, you can make little marzipan presents to put in the boats.

RICE PAPER CAKE

Ingredients
18-cm (7-in) round Victoria sandwich cake
made with 3 eggs
raspberry jam
450g (1lb) pink sugarpaste
cornflour (cornstarch)
125g (4oz) white glacé icing
coloured hundreds and thousands
icing (confectioner's) sugar, sifted

Equipment
20-cm (8-in) round cake board
rolling pin
greaseproof paper piping bag
teaspoon
17.5-cm (7-in) circle of rice paper
24-cm (1½-in) wide strips of rice paper
green, yellow, violet and pink edible food
colouring pens
sharp knife
palette knife

Cut the cake in half horizontally, spread the cut surfaces with raspberry jam using the palette knife and sandwich them together. Place the cake on the cake board, securing it in place with small dabs of glacé icing. Roll out the sugarpaste on a clean flat surface lightly dusted with sifted icing (confectioner's) sugar and shape it into a circle measuring 32.5cm (13in) in diameter. Spread the top and sides of the cake with raspberry jam, then cover the cake with the pink-coloured sugarpaste, moulding the icing smoothly over the top and sides of the cake and onto the cake board. Wash and dry your hands, dip them in cornflour and then rub them over the surface of the sugarpaste in a polishing movement to give a smooth, slightly shiny finish to the cake. Cut a piece of rice paper the correct length and width to fit round the sides of the cake, then cut it in half. Using the edible food colouring pens, draw suitable pictures on the rice paper, then position the circle on the top of the cake and the two strips around the sides, using little dabs of glacé icing to hold them in place. Using a greaseproof paper piping bag and glacé icing, pipe a decorative border around the outside edge of the cake and sprinkle hundreds and thousands onto the wet icing. If you wish, you can cover the cake board in the same way. Colour small strips of rice paper with the pens and tie into bows, then fix them to the cake with dots of glacé icing.

Rice paper pictures

Covering an iced cake with a rice paper drawing makes an unusual and unique decoration. If you aren't confident enough to pipe a special message onto a cake, you can write it on a sheet of rice paper, using edible food colouring pens, and then fix the paper in place with dots of glacé icing. You can decorate the whole of a cake in this way, or just use small cameo pictures or picture strips arranged around the sides of the cake. However, you must ensure that you use the correct pens containing edible food colouring, available from specialist shops – ordinary felt pens contain toxic ink and are not suitable. Rice paper can also be used to make sails for boats or pirate ships made from cake, adorned with suitable drawings, such as the skull and crossbones.

Children enjoy drawing their own pictures and devising special themes for their cakes, especially if they are for a celebration. As the rice paper and colouring are both edible, they could even make cakes bearing secret messages, then exchange and eat them.

SOLDIER FINGERS

Ingredients
**rectangular Victoria sponge made with 2
eggs
225g (8oz) glacé icing
red and black edible liquid food colouring
gold dragées**

Equipment
**plate or cake board
sharp knife
three mixing bowls
greaseproof paper piping bags
2 plain writing nozzles in different sizes
red ribbon**

Using the sharp knife, cut the sponge into seven equal-sized rectangles and cut slivers from the remaining scraps to form hats. Divide the icing into three bowls, ensuring that one bowl contains the most icing. Set this to one side, then colour one of the remaining bowlfuls red, and the other black. To make the soldiers, place the hat slivers at the top of five of the sponge rectangles, then pour the white icing over each of the sponge cakes and leave until set and hard. Set two rectangles to one side, then fill a piping bag with red icing and pipe the soldiers' noses, coats and trousers on the five remaining rectangles, using the larger of the two piping nozzles. Give each soldier gold dragées for buttons, then leave until set. With the black icing and the finer plain writing nozzle, pipe outlines around the soldiers and mark in the hats, boots and faces. Then pipe the outlines of their sentry boxes on the remaining two rectangles. Leave until set, then arrange on a plate or cake board and trim with a red ribbon.

Template for soldier cake

MAYPOLE CAKE

Ingredients
**15-cm (6-in) round Victoria sandwich cake
raspberry jam
500g (1lb 2oz) green-coloured buttercream
125g (4oz) green-coloured desiccated
coconut
sugar flowers**

Equipment
**22.5-cm (9-in) round cake board
sharp knife
palette knife
fork
teaspoon
No8 star nozzle
nylon piping bag
coloured drinking straw
synthetic ribbon in green, white and pink
decorative synthetic flowers**

Split the cake in half horizontally, spread the cut surfaces with raspberry jam using the palette knife and sandwich them together. Place the cake on the cake board, securing it in place with dabs of glacé icing. Wash the palette knife then use it to spread the green buttercream over the top and sides of the cake and over the cake board, keeping a little to one side for piping. Using a teaspoon, press the coloured coconut onto the board and sides of the cake to look like grass. Draw the tines of a fork across the top of the cake to make swirls in the icing. Fill a piping bag with green buttercream and, using a No8 nozzle, pipe a border of stars around the edge of the cake, then arrange sugar flowers in the icing while it is still soft. Push the drinking straw into the centre of the cake and place a circle of sugar flowers around it. Cut the ribbon into 30-cm (12-in) lengths, and curl each piece by pulling a blunt knife or the edge of a pair of scissors along its length. Secure one end of each ribbon to the top of the straw, holding each one in place with sticky tape. Anchor the other end of each ribbon to the top edge of the cake with a piped star, then place a sugar flower on top of it. Disguise the sticky tape at the top of the straw with a twist of curled ribbon, if necessary holding it in place with a tiny dot of glacé icing. Decorate with synthetic flowers.

Ribbons and bows

You can make curled ribbons to decorate a cake by pulling the blade of a blunt knife, or the closed blades of a pair of scissors, along a length of synthetic ribbon. The tauter you hold the ribbon, the curlier will be the finished result.

Placing ribbon rosettes in the centre of an iced cake gives a very simple but pretty effect. Using narrow ribbon in a colour that complements the rest of the cake decoration, shape the ribbon into loops and then tie or staple them together. If you wish, you can use more than one colour of ribbon for each rosette. To make a decoration for a candle, push the spike of a candle holder through the rosette and into the cake. However, the ribbon may be inflammable, so take care not to let the candle burn down to its base, or the rosette may catch fire.

Small bows can be made by looping a piece of ribbon twice and catching the centre with a strip of wire. Push the wire stem into the cake to hold the bow in place.

CARTOON CAKE

Ingredients
20-cm (8-in) square rich fruit cake
1kg (2 lb) marzipan
1kg (2 lb) sugarpaste
75g (3oz) icing (confectioner's)
sugar, sifted
egg white
15ml (1 tbsp) sherry
225g (8oz) royal icing
tangerine, blue, red, black and brown
edible paste food colourings
water

Equipment
40 x 30-cm (16 x 12-in) cake board
blue sugar art pen
pastry brush
piping bag
No5 star nozzle
rolling pin
tape measure
sharp knife
long carving knife
clean cosmetic sponge
pencil
tracing paper
No2 paintbrush
small plate or saucer
kitchen paper
35cm (14in) ribbon

Make a line down the middle of the cake, dividing it in two, then carefully carve the two sections so they resemble the open pages of a book. Place the cake on the board, fixing it in place with small dabs of royal icing. Cover the cake with one layer of marzipan and one of sugarpaste. Trim any excess with the sharp knife. With a long carving knife, make chopping movements along the sides of the cake to make them look like pages of a book. Using a No5 shell piping nozzle and white royal icing, pipe a shell design around the base of the cake. Leave the cake to dry out for a day before you begin to paint it. Draw your own characters or use the ones given here, then trace them onto a sheet of tracing paper and transfer them to the top of the cake, ensuring you don't smudge the lines. Using the No2 paintbrush, mix the colours with a little water on a saucer. Dab the brush on a sheet of kitchen paper before you begin to paint, so that the brush isn't too wet. Paint the body in tangerine, the balloon, tongue and braces in red, the jeans in blue, the football in brown and then the eyes, nose, mouth, balloon string and eyebrows in black. Outline the character in black and paint the details on the jeans. Leave a little white showing in the eyes and on the nose to give life to the character. Using the sugar art pen, write your greeting on the cake, making sure you don't press too hard. Place the ribbon along the centre of the cake and fix it in place by pushing it into the back of the cake with a thin-bladed knife.

Making different book cakes

There are many ways of adapting this basic idea to make a book cake for almost any occasion. For example, make an exam cake by painting or writing, with a sugar art pen, maths sums or physics formulae over the sugarpaste. You can also choose someone's favourite poem or piece of prose, write it on one side of the cake, and illustrate it on the other. To make a confirmation cake, trace over a cross made from iced lolly sticks, then fill in the outline with gold or silver edible food colouring. On the other page, inscribe the child's name and the date of their confirmation.

KANGAROO CAKE

Ingredients
25-cm (10-in) square Victoria sponge
225g (8oz) royal icing
250g (9oz) chocolate-flavoured
buttercream
red and black edible food colourings

Icing
225g (8oz) icing (confectioner's) sugar, sifted
40g (1½oz) butter
30ml (3 dessertspoons) milk
15ml (1 tbsp) golden (corn) syrup
15ml (1 tbsp) cocoa powder

Equipment
25-cm (10-in) square cake board
saucepan
4 mixing bowls
wooden spoon
sharp knife
paper template of kangaroo
wire cooling rack
piping bags
plain writing nozzle
star piping nozzle

Place the paper template (copy this from the diagram on page 80) on the cake and cut around it, using the sharp knife, then place the cake on the wire cooling rack. Place the icing (confectioner's) sugar in a mixing bowl. Put the butter, golden (corn) syrup, milk and cocoa in the saucepan and heat until the butter has melted but before the mixture begins to boil. Allow to cool slightly, then pour the mixture onto the sugar and stir well until smooth. Leave to cool again, until the icing leaves thick trails when stirred. Pour over the cake and leave until cold and set. Divide the royal icing into three mixing bowls, and colour one bowlful red and another black. Leave the third bowlful white. Place the cake on the board then, using the red icing, pipe in the boxing gloves. Use the white icing to make the eyes and the black to outline the kangaroo's limbs and baby. Using a knife, spread a small amount of the chocolate buttercream over the kangaroo's pouch, ears and throat. Finish the cake by piping a row of small chocolate buttercream stars around the bottom edge of the cake.

Chocolate icings

There are several types of chocolate icing, but here are recipes for two of the more simple ones.

Chocolate buttercream
This recipe makes enough buttercream to fill and decorate a 20-cm (8-in) sponge cake.

175g (6oz) butter or soft margarine
250g (8oz) icing (confectioner's) sugar, sifted
25g (1oz) cocoa
45ml (3 tbsp) boiling water

Dissolve the cocoa in the boiling water and allow to cool. Beat the butter or margarine until smooth and soft. Add the sifted icing (confectioner's) sugar and mix until creamy. Stir in the cooled cocoa and mix well.

Melted chocolate icing
Melted chocolate makes a quick and simple icing as it can be spread directly onto the cake.

Break a bar of baker's (compound) chocolate into squares and put them in a bowl which is sitting in a pan of very hot water. Take care not to let any water touch the chocolate or you will spoil its final appearance. Leave the chocolate in the bowl until it has melted, stirring occasionally.

Alternatively you can melt the chocolate in a microwave by placing the bowl of chocolate squares in the oven and cooking them until they have melted. Immediately the chocolate is runny, smooth it over the cake with a palette knife and leave to set. To make chocolate shapes, spread the melted chocolate onto a sheet of waxed paper until it is the thickness you require. Once it begins to harden, cut it into shapes with a sharp knife. You may find this easier if first you dip the knife in boiling water. If the shapes are not for immediate use, store them first in an airtight tin when they are completely hard.

BOY'S CHRISTENING CAKE

Ingredients
20-cm (8-in) round rich fruit cake
800g (1¾lb) marzipan
900g (2lb) sugarpaste
225g (8oz) royal icing
egg white, lightly beaten
50g (2oz) icing (confectioner's) sugar, sifted
15ml (1 tbsp) sherry
blue, red, yellow, brown and paprika edible
food colourings

Equipment
27.5-cm (11-in) round cake board
rolling pin
tape measure
patterned spoon handle or pastry pattern press
clean cosmetic sponge
sharp knife
pastry brush
greaseproof paper piping bags
No5 star nozzle
No2 paintbrush
cocktail stick
flower cutter

Place the cake upside down on the board, then cover it with one layer of marzipan and one of sugarpaste, smoothing both down with your hands. With a No5 star nozzle and royal icing, pipe a row of shells around the top and bottom edges of the cake. Knead the remaining ball of sugarpaste until it is soft and easy to work with, then mould 40g (1½oz) of the paste into an oblong shape, and pinch the sides with your fingers to thin them out. Press a patterned spoon handle or a pastry pattern press around the sides to imprint a pattern in the sugarpaste. This makes the pillow. Now roll out some more sugarpaste to a thickness of 3mm (6in), and cut out an 11.25-cm (4½-in) square. Press the same spoon handle or pastry press around the edges of the square to make the quilt. With a sharp knife, mark out 5 lines along the quilt and 5 lines down it, making 25 squares in all. To make the baby's head, tint 15g (½oz) of sugarpaste with a scant amount of paprika edible food colouring, keep a tiny piece to one side and shape the rest into a ball, lightly flattening the top half of one side. Mould the tiny piece of sugarpaste into a ball, then stick onto the rounded side of the head, with a dab of water, to make the nose. Paint on the hair and eyelashes using liquid brown edible food colouring and a dampened paintbrush. Mark out the mouth with the end of a cocktail stick and fill in the shape with red edible food colouring. Make an indentation in the pillow and attach the head to it with a little water, then place it on the cake, using more water to hold it in place. Use a thick sausage of sugarpaste for the body, then place this on the cake, joining it at the head. Place the quilt over the body, fixing it in place with a little water, then shape the corners of the quilt so it doesn't look flat. With the blue colouring, paint a design on each of the squares in turn. Mix the colouring with varying amounts of water to get different shades of blue, but remember to dab the brush onto some kitchen paper to remove any excess water before painting on the quilt, or the colour may run. Colour some sugarpaste blue, then roll it out and cut out 13 flowers with the flower cutter. Place three of the flowers around the pillow and ten evenly around the sides of the cake. Pipe a yellow dot of royal icing in the centre of each flower, then with the No5 nozzle, pipe a white icing star between each flower arranged around the sides of the cake.

Making a get-well cake

To transform this from a christening into a get-well cake, turn down the corners of the mouth of the patient to give an unhappy expression. Make a small square of sugarpaste and paint a zig-zag line on it to represent a temperature chart. Write 'Get well' on the cake and change the colours to pink if the recipient is a girl.

GIRL'S CHRISTENING CAKE

Ingredients
20-cm (8-in) hexagonal rich fruit cake
800g (1¾lb) marzipan
800g (1¾lb) pink sugarpaste
250g (9oz) white sugarpaste
225g (8oz) white royal icing
egg white
50g (2oz) icing (confectioner's) sugar, sifted
15ml (1 tbsp) sherry
pink and yellow edible food pastes
glass of clean water
yellow royal icing

Equipment
25-cm (10-in) hexagonal cake board
dressmakers' pins

pastry brush
rolling pin
tape measure
sharp knife
cosmetic sponge
cellophane
piping bags
No0 piping nozzle
No2 writing nozzle
7.5-cm (3-in) round fluted pastry cutter
2.5-cm (1-in) round plain cutter or lid
cocktail stick (wooden toothpick)
flower cutter
clean damp tea towel
paintbrush
lace pattern traced from printed drawing
bootee template

Place the lace pattern on a board and pin the cellophane paper over it. Using the No0 nozzle and white royal icing, trace over the outline onto the cellophane. Begin with the straight line at the top of the bootee, then trace the shape of the bootee and finally the bow. Make sure that all the piped lines touch at the correct points to give the lace strength. You will need 36 pieces of lace, or 18 pairs of bootees, but it is a good idea to pipe extra to allow for breakages. Leave to dry. Cover the cake with a layer of marzipan followed by a layer of pink sugarpaste. To make the frill, dust the working surface with a very little sifted icing (confectioner's) sugar – using too much will make the sugarpaste dry out and crack. Roll out 75g (3oz) of white sugarpaste until it is paper-thin, then cut out five rounds with the 7.5-cm (3-in) round fluted pastry cutter. Cut out the centre of each circle with the 2.5-cm (1-in) pastry cutter. Work on one piece at a time and keep the rest covered under a clean damp tea towel. Make a cut on one side of the round and open it out to make a semi-circular shape then, using your finger, roll a cocktail stick (wooden toothpick) along the scalloped edge until it forms a frill. If the stick cuts into the icing instead of rolling along the top, the icing is too thick and you will have to start again. Lift up the frill and place it on your palm with the wrong side uppermost. Using the paintbrush, brush a little water along the top edge of the frill and then firmly attach it in a straight line to one side of the cake, so that the frill's base just touches the cake board. Repeat this all round the cake until all six sides have a white frill. Take another 75g (3oz) of sugarpaste, colour it a very pale pink and then repeat the procedure for the first row of frills, this time positioning them about 12mm (½in) higher up the cake. For the top frill, colour the remaining 75g (3oz) of sugarpaste the

same colour as the cake. When you have made the frill, fold down each side to give a neat edge. Attach the frill to the side of the cake in the usual way, about 12mm (½in) higher than the second row, but let it form a curve instead of a straight line. Working anti-clockwise, place the edge of the second frill on top of the right-hand point of the first frill. Continue in this way round the cake until you reach the last frill, when you should lift up the left-hand point of the first frill and place the right-hand point of the last frill underneath it. This will make it difficult to see where the frills are joined. Cut out a cardboard template of the bootee and roll out some white sugarpaste until it is about 3mm (6in) thick. Now cut out one bootee shape with a sharp knife, then invert the template and cut out another bootee, to give one left and one right foot. Arrange them on the top of the cake, fixing them in place with a little water. With the No2 nozzle and a little royal icing coloured dark pink, pipe bows onto the bootees and write the child's name on the cake. Colour 15g (½oz) of sugarpaste slightly darker than the base of the cake, roll out and cut out four flowers, then attach these to the cake with a little water. Colour a little royal icing yellow, and use to pipe dots in the centre of each flower. Above the centre of each frill, press the flower cutter into the sugarpaste to form an outline, then ice over the marks with white royal icing and a No0 nozzle. Pipe four white dots either side of each flower and a yellow dot in its centre. Gently detach the lace bootees from the waxed paper, then pipe a line of white icing along the top edge of each frill. Place one pair of bootees in the centre of each frill and one pair either side of them, as shown in the photograph. Pipe one white dot between the paired bootees and three white dots between each pair of bootees.

44

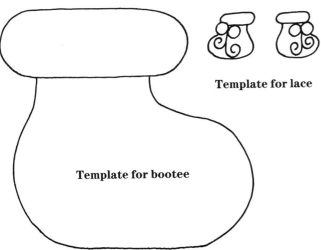

Template for lace

Template for bootee

Successful lace work

Lace work is not as difficult as it looks if you remember to follow some simple guidelines.

You will get the best results by using freshly-beaten royal icing. It should be soft enough to pipe easily, but not so soft that it doesn't hold its shape. Always make sure that the lines touch at the points shown in the pattern, as this is what gives the lace its strength. If you want to use coloured icing, ensure that the colouring doesn't contain glycerol, as this will prevent the icing setting. Always pipe more pieces of lace than you will need to allow for breakages. Ensure that you only handle the finished pieces of lace with your fingers, not a pair of tweezers, as these are liable to make the lace pieces break.

HAPPY MOTHER'S DAY!

Ingredients
rich fruit cake mixture cooked in a 1.2-litre
(2-pint) pudding basin
450g (1lb) marzipan
egg white, lightly beaten
450g (1lb) sugarpaste
50g (2oz) icing (confectioner's) sugar, sifted
15ml (1 tbsp) sherry
225g (8oz) royal icing
pink edible paste food colouring

Equipment
22.5-cm (9-in) round cake board
20-cm (8-in) special cake doll
7.5-cm (3-in) pastry cutter
½ metre (½ yard) net or tulle
needle and cotton
No0 writing nozzle
scissors
½ metre (½ yard) ribbon
small flower cutter
paintbrush

Place the cake in the centre of the cake board. Push the doll's trunk through the centre of the cake – if her waist sits above the top of the cake, you will have to build up the cake to this level, using marzipan. Smooth this so that it follows the curved shape of the cake. Remove the doll. Cover the cake with marzipan, then trim off any excess at the base of the cake and trim the marzipan from the hole in which the doll will sit. Put a small amount of sugarpaste to one side, then colour the rest pale pink and knead well, ensuring that the colour is evenly distributed and there are no streaks and cover the cake with a layer of sugarpaste. Push the doll into the top of the cake and press the sugarpaste around her waist to hold her in place. Take a piece of the white sugarpaste and roll it out until it is approximately 11.25cm (4½in) long and 2.5cm (1in) wide, to make her bodice. Brush a little egg white over her trunk and stick on the sugarpaste, having first lifted up her arms. Arrange the join of the bodice in the centre of her back, trimming off any overlapping paste with a sharp knife to make a neat seam. Leave the cake in a cool place for 24 hours to allow the sugarpaste to become firm. Cut out a circle of net 37.5cm (15in) in diameter, then cut out a 5-cm (2-in) diameter hole in the centre of that. Sew two rows of tacking stitches near the edge of the central hole, then drop the skirt over the doll's head and gather it neatly around her waist by gently pulling tight the two strands of cotton. If the net sticks out too much, pin around the bottom edge of the dress and leave for a day. Wrap a piece of ribbon around the doll's waist, tying it in a bow at the back and letting the two ends of ribbon hang down. Pipe dots and flowers over her net skirt with royal icing and a No0 nozzle, then pipe dots over the bodice and around the doll's neck to make a necklace, and around her wrist to make a bracelet. With the 7.5-cm (3-in) round pastry cutter, cut a circle out of a rolled-out piece of sugarpaste, then attach it to the doll's head with dabs of royal icing and shape into a hat. Cut out three sugarpaste flowers, mould into shape and place in the doll's hand, fixing them in position with a little royal icing.

Ingredients
Victoria sandwich mixture made with 2 or 3 eggs, according to the size of the mould
250g (8oz) yellow glacé icing
green and red piping gel

Equipment
fish-shaped mould, greased and dusted with flour
wooden board 50 x 15cm (20 x 6in), covered in aluminium foil
bowl
knife
spoon
greaseproof paper piping bag
wire cooling rack

Fill the fish-shaped mould with Victoria sandwich mixture and bake until cooked. Turn the cooked cake onto the wire rack and leave until cold. Spoon some of the yellow glacé icing over the cake until it is completely covered, then leave to dry. Divide the remaining glacé icing in two, place half in the piping bag and pipe scales and contours onto the fish. Allow to dry. Carefully place the fish on the foil-covered board, holding it in place with dabs of glacé icing. Fill the piping bag with the rest of the icing and pipe a line around the base of the fish. Piping the green piping gel straight from the tube or bottle, fill in the scales and contours of the fish. Use red piping gel to draw the eye and first line of scales. You can also use the gel to draw marine designs, such as weed, on the foil.

Piping gel

Decorating a cake with piping gel is not only quick and easy but also very effective. It is sold clear or in a variety of colours – red, yellow, green and blue – and can be piped directly from the tube or bottle onto the cake. However, because the gel is clear, if it is piped directly onto the surface of a plain cake, the colour of the cake will show through. You will achieve a more satisfactory effect by piping the gel onto a base of dry glacé icing. If the surface of the cake is not flat, the gel can slide off, as it doesn't set hard. Anchor it in place with a firm wall of piped glacé icing.

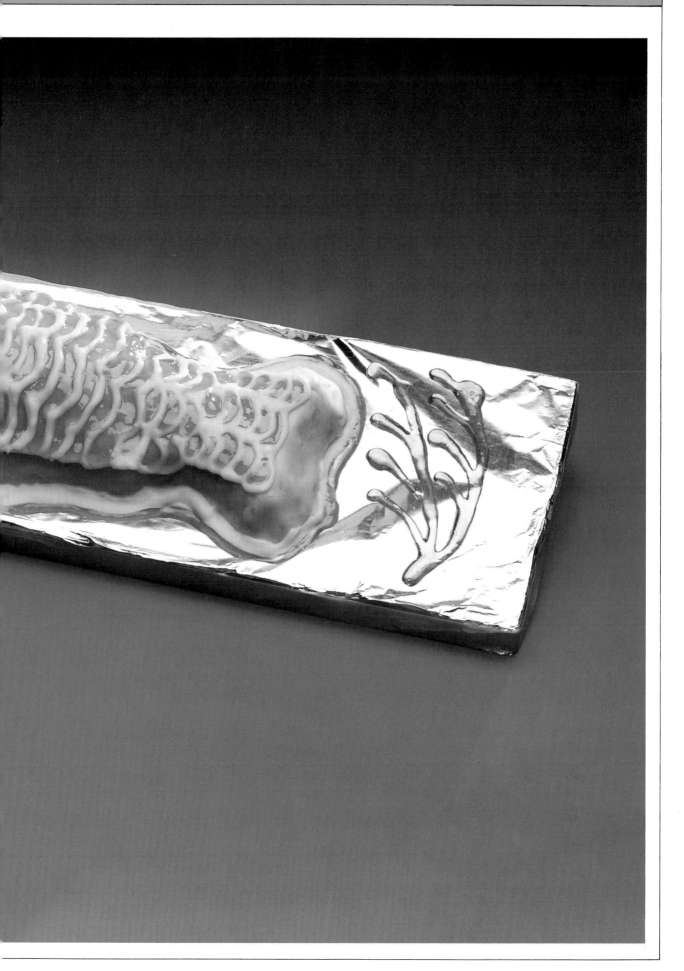

ENGAGEMENT CAKE

Ingredients
700g (1½lb) rich fruit cake baked in a
17.5-cm (7-in) heart-shaped tin (pan)
450g (1lb) marzipan
700g (1½lb) royal icing
blue petal dust
snow flake sparkle
French pink edible food colouring
10ml (2 tsp) glycerine

Equipment
25-cm (10-in) heart-shaped cake board
turntable
pink and blue ribbons
length of pink ribbon if desired
piping bags
No43 star nozzle
No1 writing nozzle
No3 writing nozzle

Place the cake in the centre of the cake board and secure in position with small dabs of royal icing. Cover the cake and board with a layer of marzipan, then apply three thin coats of pale pink royal icing, allowing each one to dry hard before applying the next. Make the run-out butterflies and flowers (see feature), and allow to set for at least two days. Dust the butterfly wings with blue petal dust and paint by hand if wished. Working from the centre of the heart to the bottom point, pipe a line of simple shells around one top edge of the cake, using a star nozzle and deep pink royal icing. Repeat around the other half, making the shells meet at both ends. Now pipe along the base of the cake in the same way. Allow to dry. With a No1 writing nozzle and white royal icing, and again starting at the centre of the heart, pipe a loop joining every alternate shell along the top edge of the cake, then leave to dry. Now repeat the process, this time piping loops between the shells that you avoided first time round. Pipe loops along the base of the cake, joining up every shell, then pipe dots between each shell on the sides of the cake and leave to dry. With pale green royal icing and the No3 writing nozzle, pipe the stems and leaves of the flowers on the top of the cake, then place the run-out flowers in position, fixing them to the cake top with tiny dabs of royal icing. Pipe the white buds directly onto the surface of the cake, using white royal icing and a No5 nozzle. Choose the position of the butterflies, then with a No3 tube and pale blue royal icing, pipe the bodies onto the cake top, gently place the wings in the wet icing and allow to dry. If they won't stand up,

carefully place a small piece of cosmetic sponge on the outer side of each wing and remove when the icing has dried. Measure the circumference of the cake, then make a template this size. Divide it into 16 sections and cut a small hole in the centre of each section. Gently wrap this around the cake and mark the position of each hole by making a pin prick in the surface of the cake. Pipe alternate blue dots and pink heart shapes around the sides of the cake, using the pin pricks as a guide to their position. To make the hearts, use a No3 piping nozzle and pipe one half of the heart with pressure piping, then pipe in the other half. Disguise the edge of the cake board by covering it with a length of pink ribbon, held in place with dabs of royal icing.

Making run-outs

To make a run-out flower, first draw the shape. Ensure that you form clear, strong lines that are easy to follow. Place the drawings on a board, cover with a sheet of cellophane and pin in place, securing the drawing at the same time – it must not be able to move about or the icing will crack. Pipe over the outlines of the flower in royal icing with a No0 writing nozzle, having first checked the consistency of the icing – it should be fairly stiff. Now fill in the shape with more royal icing, having thinned it down with cold water and added 15ml (3 tsp) powdered egg white to give added strength.

To make a run-out butterfly, prepare the outlines of the wings following the flower instructions. Fill in the icing halfway down each wing, and brush in the rest of the icing to make the wings very thin. Leave to dry, then brush with colour and sparkle.

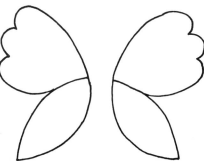

Template for butterfly wing

Template for butterfly body

Template for flower

CLASSIC WEDDING CAKE

Ingredients
1 22.5-cm (9-in) and 1 17.5-cm (7-in) heart-
shaped rich fruit cake
1.4kg (3lb) marzipan
1.8kg (4lb) royal icing

Equipment
1 25-cm (10-in) heart-shaped cake board
1 30-cm (12-in) heart-shaped cake board
turntable
scraper with a straight edge
No43 star nozzle
No58 petal nozzle
No1 writing nozzle
greaseproof paper
dressmaker's pin
3½ metres (4 yards) ribbon
3 cake tier supports
vase containing fresh flowers

Ideally, the cakes should be allowed to mature for about 10 weeks before the wedding, so wrap them well in greaseproof paper and aluminium foil, and store in a cool place. Two to three weeks before the wedding, cover the cakes with marzipan, then place them on the boards, fixing them in position with dabs of royal icing, and apply the first of four coats of royal icing. Apply one coat of icing a day to each cake, ensuring that you finish at least one week before the wedding to give the icing time to become completely firm. To decorate the cakes, make a greaseproof paper template of each cake, then divide the smaller one into 12 sections, and the larger into 16 sections. Place the templates around the cakes and prick out the sections with a pin. With a No43 nozzle and royal icing, pipe scrolls around the top of each cake, working anticlockwise from the centre of the heart to the point, and then pipe clockwise down the other side of the cake, making each scroll start on the top of the cake and end by slightly overlapping the edge. Using the No1 nozzle, overpipe each scroll with two lines slightly curved into an S-shape. With the No58 petal nozzle and the thick side touching the side of the cake, pipe a frill beneath each scroll, working the piping bag up and down to form the pleats. Using the No1 tube again, pipe lines along the top of each cake following the shape of the scrolls. Pipe the bottom borders of the cakes with the No43 nozzle, first piping a line of large shells, and then piping a line of smaller shells above it. With the No1 nozzle, pipe loops to join up the small shells, then pipe dots on the side of each cake between the small shells. Pipe a loop underneath each scroll on the side of each cake, then pipe three graduated dots beneath the join of each loop. Leave until completely dry, then wrap a white ribbon around each cake and tie in a bow. You can also cover the edges of each cake board with more ribbon, held in place with small dabs of royal icing and neatly joined at the centre of the heart. To assemble the cake, place three cake pillars in the centre of the largest cake, arranging two at the back and one at the front. Use four pillars per layer if assembling a square cake. Finish the cake by placing a small vase of fresh flowers, to match the bride's bouquet, on the top tier. The florist who makes the bouquet should do this.

HAPPY ANNIVERSARY!

Ingredients
20-cm (8-in) square rich fruit cake
900g-1.1kg (2-2½lb) marzipan
1.1kg (2½lb) royal icing
mauve edible food colouring
warmed sieved apricot jam

Equipment
27.5-cm (11-in) square cake board
turntable
metal straight edge
scraper knife
greaseproof paper
dressmaker's pin
piping bags
No43 star nozzle
No46 star nozzle
No1 writing nozzle
crystallized flowers
2m (2 yards) white ribbon, 6mm (¼in) wide
1m (1 yard) white ribbon, 3mm (6in) wide

Spread the top and sides of the cake with the apricot jam, and then a layer of marzipan. Place the cake on the board, holding it in place with dots of royal icing. Cover the cake and board with three thin coats of mauve-coloured royal icing, allowing each coat to dry before applying the next. Trace a 14cm (5½in) square onto a sheet of greaseproof paper, then place over the top of the cake and prick out the diamond outline with a pin. With white royal icing and the No1 piping nozzle, pipe in the diamond shape. Now pipe neat rows of straight lines from the diamond outline to the edge of the cake and allow to dry before piping neat straight rows across the first lines, to form a criss-cross pattern. Using the No43 nozzle and white royal icing, pipe shells around the top edges of the cake. Now, using the No46 nozzle, fill a piping bag with both colours of icing, ranging the white down one side and the mauve down the other. Pipe a border of large upward-pointing shells around the base of the cake and a double row of shells up each corner, to give a two-tone effect. With the No43 nozzle and mauve and white icing, pipe a row of downward-pointing shells along the top of the lower border of large shells. Join the smaller shells with loops of white icing using the No1 nozzle and pipe a row of dots above the bottom border of shells and up the sides of the cake. Pipe loops of stars around the four sides of the cake with the No43 nozzle, making them graduate in size as you work towards the corners. Pipe a line of dots on the cake and join the shells with white loops as before. Fill in the centre diamond with tiny white spots, which can also be piped on the sides if wished. Make four bows from the narrow ribbon and stick them on the corners of the cake with dabs of icing. Trim the edges of the cake board with the wider ribbon and arrange the crystallized flowers and marzipan stems on the top of the cake.

Making crystallized flowers

Ingredients
fresh flowers
petal dust
caster (superfine) sugar
1 egg white
green marzipan

Place the egg white in a bowl and lightly whisk. Mix the petal dust with the sugar and place in a bowl. Dip the clean, dry flowers in the egg white, making sure that all the petals are immersed. Brush off any excess egg white, then dip the flowers in the coloured sugar and leave to dry. Make the stems of the flowers from long thin sausages of green marzipan.

SIMNEL CAKE

Ingredients
rich or light fruit cake mixture
700g (1½lb) marzipan
225g (8oz) glacé icing
warmed sieved apricot jam
edible food colouring
lemon flavouring

Equipment
20-cm (8-in) round cake tin (pan), greased
and lined
22.5-cm (9-in) cake board
rolling pan
wire cooling rack
1½ metres (1½ yards) ribbon

Pour half the cake mixture into the greased and lined tin (pan), then roll out one-third of the marzipan and cut into a circle the same size as the tin and place on top of the cake mixture. Fill the tin with the rest of the mixture and bake. Leave to cool in the tin for a few minutes, then turn out onto a wire rack, remove the lining paper and leave until cold. Make the daffodils with lemon-flavoured marzipan (see feature). Trim the top of the cake if it is very uneven, to give a flat surface, then spread the top of the cake with the warmed sieved apricot jam. Roll out another third of the marzipan into a 20-cm (8-in) circle and place on top of the cake. Using the last third of marzipan, roll it into two round, thin lengths. Twist these into a rope and place around the top edge of the cake, trimming to fit. Place the cake under a hot grill until the marzipan is golden brown. Leave until cold. Pour the melted warm fondant or glacé icing into the centre of the cake, spread it in an even layer and leave for two hours until completely set. Place the cake in the centre of the cake board, then arrange the daffodils on top of the cake and wrap the ribbon around the side, tying it in a large bow.

Making marzipan daffodils

It is much easier than it looks to make daffodils from marzipan, and they give a very professional finish to a cake. Flavour some marzipan with lemon flavouring, then divide into two balls and colour one pale yellow and the other dark yellow. Roll a teardrop shape from a walnut-sized piece of pale yellow marzipan, flatten one end and place on a cocktail stick (wooden toothpick). To open the throat of the flower, cut six petals with a sharp knife, tease them open and leave to dry. Take a piece of dark yellow marzipan the size of a peanut and roll it into a teardrop shape, then flatten one end. Push your finger into the marzipan until you form a cone, then place this in the centre of the open petals of the outer trumpet. With green-coloured royal icing, pipe green stamens inside the dark yellow cone and leave until dry, then place the flower on the cake and pipe long green stems with the royal icing or make stems by rolling long thin green sausages of marzipan.

EASTER BUNNY CAKE

Ingredients
sponge cake mixture made from 4 eggs
350g (12oz) sugarpaste
pink, blue, green and black edible liquid
food colouring
700g (1½lb) buttercream
boiled water

Equipment
novelty tin in shape of a rabbit
household string
fine skewer
wire cooling rack
piping bag
No13 nozzle
No3 nozzle

Grease the tin (pan) halves, ensuring that all the hollows and corners are well coated, then sprinkle flour into each half to cover all the surfaces and shake out. Heat the oven to 170°C (325°F) Gas Mark 3. Completely fill the front half of the tin with the cake mixture, then put the back half in place. Tie the tins tightly together in two places with household string to prevent the cake mixture oozing out as it cooks. Bake in the middle of the oven for 20-30 minutes, testing by inserting a fine skewer in the vent hole at the top of the tin. If it comes out clean, the cake is cooked. Remove the cake from the oven and allow to cool in the tins for a few minutes, then untie the string and remove the top half of the tin. When the cake is completely cold, remove the other half of the tin. Leave for at least four hours before decorating. Cover the cake board with a layer of green-coloured sugarpaste, then place the rabbit in the centre of the board. Colour some buttercream pink, then pipe lines to define the legs and mouth using a No3 nozzle. Cut out ovals of pink sugarpaste for the nose and the insides of the ears and fix in position with a little boiled water. To make the rabbit's eyes, colour some sugarpaste pale blue and fix in place with boiled water. Paint in the pupils with black liquid edible food colouring. Make a carrot from some sugarpaste coloured orange, and score its surface with a sharp knife to make indentations. Using a No13 nozzle and uncoloured buttercream, pipe stars over the whole of the rabbit's body, working in neat horizontal rows so that the surface of the cake can't be seen. Now, using pink buttercream, pipe in a pink tail made from rows of stars. Finish the rabbit by fixing a sugar flower between its ears and giving it two front teeth made from white buttercream.

EASTER EGG BASKET

Ingredients
**17.5-cm (7-in) round sponge cake or
purchased flan case
225g (8oz) peach-coloured royal icing
8 chocolate eggs, decorated**

Equipment
**handle from a small wicker basket
25-cm (10-in) oval cake board
large piping bag
No37 basket weave nozzle
2m (2 yards) peach-coloured ribbon, 3mm
(⅛in) wide
75cm (24in) broderie anglaise
75cm (24in) peach-coloured ribbon, 6mm
(¼in) wide**

Bend the wicker basket handle to fit the cake, place in position and fix with royal icing. Place the cake on the board. Using the No37 nozzle and the royal icing, pipe round the cake to create the basket-weave effect. Start at the bottom edge of the cake and pipe a 2.5-cm (1-in) length, then lift the nozzle quickly. Pipe another length next to the first one, so that they appear to overlap. Continue in this way all round the cake until you have piped four rows of basket weave, then allow to dry for about 30 minutes. Wrap the 3-mm (⅛-in) wide ribbon around the basket handle and finish with a bow on one side. Thread the thicker ribbon through the broderie anglaise then use it to trim the board. Fill the basket with the decorated eggs.

Decorating chocolate eggs

Homemade and purchased Easter eggs can be decorated with piped royal icing. To make Easter eggs, choose one of the many chocolate moulds available and clean thoroughly with cotton wool. Melt baker's (compound) chocolate and pour into the mould. Leave until completely set, then turn out. To join the two halves, very briefly place one half on a heated baking tray, then quickly press onto the other half. To decorate the eggs, either fasten each one to the work surface with a dab of royal icing or place in an egg cup. Chocolate shows fingerprints if handled too much, so try to work without touching the eggs. Pipe on the designs using brightly coloured icing and small nozzles. Geometric designs, flowers and faces are all suitable. You can also decorate eggs with piped melted chocolate. Use a double-thickness piping bag and cut off the end to the size of a No2 nozzle. Choose a contrasting colour of chocolate to that of the eggs, or use white baker's chocolate, which can be coloured with oil-based confectioner's colours.

SNOWSCENE CAKE

Ingredients
15-cm (6-in) round rich fruit cake
warmed sieved apricot jam
450g (1lb) marzipan
sifted icing (confectioner's) sugar
450g (1lb) white royal icing
snowmen made from sugarpaste (see feature)

Equipment
20-cm (8-in) round cake board
pastry brush
palette or dinner knife
rolling pin
bowl
foil Christmas cake ribbon
plastic robin and holly decorations

Cover the cake with the marzipan, then leave to dry for a few days. Place the cake in the centre of the cake board, securing it in position with a few dabs of royal icing. Spread the remaining icing over the cake with a palette or dinner knife then, using the flat edge of the knife, pull the icing into rough peaks. Allow to dry overnight. Fix the coloured foil ribbon around the cake, securing the join with a dot of royal icing. Arrange the snowmen, plastic robin and holly on top of the cake, fixing them in place with dabs of icing.

Making the sugarpaste snowmen

You can turn even the simplest Christmas cake into something special by making your own decorations. Here, the snowmen are made from sugarpaste. This quantity is enough to make four 5-cm (2-in) high figures.

250g (8oz) white sugarpaste
red and brown food colouring
a few currants
skewer

To make each snowman, mould a piece of sugarpaste into an oval shape about 2.5-4cm (1-1½in) high. Roll out a ball of sugarpaste to form the head and join together to make a snowman shape. Colour some sugarpaste red and some brown. Roll the red sugarpaste into a sausage shape for the scarf and wrap it around the snowman's neck. Mould the brown sugarpaste into a hat and press a small piece into the head to make a moustache, using a skewer. To make the buttons, press two currants into the body, and form the eyes by making two holes in the head with the skewer. Put a drop of red colouring in each eye and leave to dry.

CHRISTMAS TREE CAKE

Ingredients
35.5 x 25.5 x 4-cm (14 x 10 x 1½-in)
slab of gingerbread or butter
sponge cake
175g (6oz) thick white glacé icing
125g (4oz) slightly runny green glacé icing
350g (12oz) green buttercream
gold, silver and red dragées

Equipment
small sharp knife
greaseproof paper
pencil
pins
palette knife
3 piping bags
No2 plain writing nozzle
skewer
No8 star piping nozzle
4 ribbon rosettes

Cut the gingerbread or butter sponge cake into a Christmas tree shape with a small, sharp knife. You can cut the cake freehand, but you may find it easier to draw the required shape on a sheet of greaseproof paper, then pin this template on the cake and cut around it. With a palette knife, spread the thick white glacé icing over the top of the cake and leave for five minutes to set slightly. Then with the No2 nozzle and runny green glacé icing, pipe lines down the length of the cake, about 20mm (¾in) apart. Before the icing has set, draw lines at right angles over the green icing with the skewer. Decorate with gold, silver and red dragées. Insert the No8 star nozzle into a piping bag and fill it with green buttercream. Pipe rows of stars along the sides of the cake. Place one ribbon rosette at the top of the tree and three along its base to complete the decoration.

CHRISTMAS CANDLE CAKE

Ingredients
175g (6oz) rich fruit cake cooked in 2 tins,
10cm (4in) in diameter (pineapple ring tins are ideal)
warmed sieved apricot jam
egg white
700g (1½lb) marzipan
225g (8oz) white royal icing
50g (2oz) icing (confectioner's) sugar, sifted

Equipment
22.5-cm (9-in) round cake board
tape measure
rolling pin
sharp knife
scissors
melon yellow, gooseberry green and red
paste food colours
pastry brush
holly leaf cutter or card template of holly
leaf

Sandwich the two cakes together with apricot jam and fill any gaps or holes with small pieces of marzipan. Measure the circumference and height of the cakes, adding 5cm (2in) to the height to cover the top of the cake – your final measurements should be about 32.5 x 20cm (13 x 8in). Roll out the marzipan to the correct size and wrap it around the cake. Remove any overlap with a sharp knife and mould the two cut edges together with your fingers until the join is smooth. Cut off the marzipan at the bottom of the cake with a clean pair of scissors and smooth down any rough edges with your fingers. Press the marzipan around the top of the cake until it is completely covered, then cut off any excess and smooth it down with your fingers. Check that your hands are free from cake crumbs, then roll the cake over the clean flat surface to remove any lumps in the marzipan. Now place the cake upright on the cake

board, securing it in place with dabs of royal icing. To make the candle flame, take 50g (2oz) yellow-coloured marzipan. Shape it into a cone, then press it onto the working surface to make a flat flame shape. Paint the middle of each side of the flame with red edible food colouring, making the edges of the flame lighter than the centre, and allow to dry. Make a well with your hand in the centre of the cake top, then pour in the royal icing and let it drip down the sides of the cake, like wax on a candle. Place the flame in the icing while it is still wet. Colour 25g (1oz) of the marzipan green and roll it out until quite thin. Using the holly leaf template or cutters, cut out 12 leaves. Colour 15g (½oz) of the marzipan red and make some berries. Arrange the leaves and berries around the bottom of the candle, giving each leaf a twist to make it more life-like and then sprinkling it with sifted icing (confectioner's) sugar.

Template for holly leaf

Making a candle

To make a coloured candle, work red or green edible food colouring into the marzipan before rolling it out. If it is very sticky or your hands are very warm, wear thin surgical gloves while moulding the marzipan. If the baked cakes are an odd shape, make sure that the marzipan covering evens them up. If using tin cans, remove any sharp edges and then wash and dry them thoroughly. Make sure they are well-lined with greased greaseproof paper, and push the paper well into the corners.

CHRISTMAS COOKIES

Ingredients
Biscuits
175g (6oz) butter
125g (4oz) caster (superfine) sugar
2 egg yolks
15-30ml (1-2 tbsp) water
175g (6oz) plain (all-purpose) flour, sifted
5ml (1 tsp) baking powder
few drops vanilla essence
salt

Icing
1 egg white
225g (8oz) icing (confectioner's)
sugar, sifted
edible liquid food colouring

Decorations
coloured ribbons
coloured dragées

Equipment
greased baking sheet
mixing bowl
wooden spoon or electric mixer
rolling pin
biscuit cutters
skewer
wire cooling rack
egg whisk
piping bag
No1 writing nozzle

Heat the oven to 180°C (350°F) Gas Mark 5. Cream together the butter and sugar in the mixing bowl, then add the egg yolk and water and flavour with a few drops of vanilla essence. Stir the sifted flour, baking powder and salt into the mixture to make a dough, adding a little more water if the consistency is too dry. Turn the dough onto a lightly floured board and knead until it is smooth. Roll out until the mixture is about 12mm (½in) thick and cut into shapes with the cutters. Make a hole in one end of each biscuit with the skewer. Place the biscuits on the greased baking sheet and bake for 12-15 minutes, then leave on a wire rack until cold. In the meantime, make the icing by whisking the egg white until it is frothy, then gradually add the sifted icing (confectioner's) sugar until the icing is the desired consistency – it should be able to flow from the tube and hold its shape. Divide the icing in two, and colour half of it with edible liquid food colouring. When the biscuits are quite cold, ice and decorate them with piping. Leave to dry, then thread ribbon through the holes. They can then be tied on a Christmas tree or hung from a mantelpiece.

GINGERBREAD COTTAGE

Ingredients

Gingerbread
575g (1¼lb) self-raising flour, sifted
45ml (3 tbsp) ground ginger
25ml (1½ tbsp) mixed spice
225g (8oz) caster (superfine) sugar
175g (6oz) butter
2 eggs
120ml (8 tbsp) golden (corn) syrup
30ml (2 tbsp) black treacle

Icing
1 egg white
225g (8oz) icing (confectioner's) sugar, sifted
edible liquid food colouring

Sugar syrup
225g (8oz) granulated sugar
150ml (¼ pint) water
lemon juice

Decorations
sugar flowers
cake board

Equipment
greased baking sheet
mixing bowl
wooden spoon or electric mixer
jug
polythene bag
rolling pin
aluminium foil
egg whisk
saucepan
sugar thermometer
pastry brush
25-cm (10-in) square cake board

Mix together the flour, spices and sugar, then cut the butter into the mixture and rub it in with your fingertips. Mix the eggs, golden syrup and treacle in a jug, then add a little of this at a time to the flour and butter to form a dough. Knead the mixture until it is smooth, then wrap in a polythene bag and leave in the fridge for 35 minutes to rest. Heat the oven to 170°C (325°F) Gas Mark 3. Roll out the gingerbread on a floured board until it is 6mm (¼in) thick. Use paper templates to cut out the walls and roof sections. The two roof pieces should each measure 17.5cm (7in) x 17.5cm (7in), the two side sections should each be 17.5cm (7in) x 12.5cm (5in) and the front and back of the house should measure 12.5cm (5in) x 20cm (8in) x 13.75cm (5½in). If the mixture is too moist, roll it out straight on to a sheet of aluminium foil, then place this on the greased baking sheet. Otherwise, cut the pieces out on the board and place them on the greased baking sheet. Bake in the oven for about 15 minutes, then leave until cold. If you have used foil, don't peel it off until the gingerbread is completely cold. To make the royal icing, whisk the egg white until it is frothy, then beat in the sifted icing (confectioner's) sugar until the icing holds its shape. Decorate each piece of gingerbread with royal icing and a No0 writing nozzle, piping on loops for the roof, and doors and windows for the walls. Leave to dry. To make the sugar syrup, dissolve the sugar in the water, add a squeeze of lemon juice and heat gently. Slowly bring the mixture to the boil, then boil without stirring until the sugar thermometer reads 137°C (280°F). Use the sugar syrup to stick the bottom edges of the walls to the cake board. Paint the edges of the walls and the roof with syrup and assemble the house piece by piece. Finish the house by piping icing around the base of the cake and along the centre of the roof, piping green royal icing stems up the sides of the house and fixing sugar flowers above them.

ALTERNATIVE CAKE RECIPES

Try these recipes if you can't eat ordinary cakes, you're on a special diet or if you want a change from the traditional rich fruit and sponge cakes.

Eggless cake

This unusual cake is Greek in origin and was devised to be eaten during Lent, when dairy food was not allowed. It also has no sugar, but for all that is very good to eat.

Ingredients
200g (7oz) wholewheat self-raising flour
2.5ml (½ tsp) bicarbonate of soda
75g (3oz) raisins
25g (1oz) walnuts, chopped
230ml (8 fl oz) pure orange juice
60ml (4 tbsp) tahini
60ml (4 tbsp) clear honey

Equipment
20-cm (8-in) round tin (pan), greased and lined
mixing bowl
wooden spoon or electric mixer
wire cooling rack

Heat the oven to 180°C (350°F) Gas Mark 4. Mix together the flour, bicarbonate of soda, raisins and nuts. Beat together the orange juice, tahini and honey, then stir the liquid into the dry ingredients and mix well until smooth. Pour into the prepared tin (pan) and bake for 35-40 minutes until firm to the touch. Allow to cool slightly in the tin, then turn out and leave on the wire rack until cold.

Carob cake

If you want a chocolate cake but don't like using chocolate, try this recipe and see if you can taste the difference.

Ingredients
225g (8oz) self-raising flour, sifted
75g (3oz) margarine or butter
125g (4oz) soft demerara sugar
15ml (1 tbsp) carob powder
a little water or soya milk for mixing

Equipment
17.5-cm (7-in) round cake tin (pan), greased and lined
mixing bowl
wooden spoon or electric mixer
wire cooling rack

Heat the oven to 160°C (325°F) Gas Mark 3. Place all the dry ingredients in the mixing bowl and rub in the margarine or butter. Mix to a firm dough with a little water or soya milk. Spoon into the prepared tin (pan) and bake for about 35 minutes or until the cake is springy to the touch. Allow to cool in the tin for a few minutes, then turn out on the wire rack, remove the lining paper and leave until completely cold.

Gluten-free cake

Make this rich fruit cake if you are not able to eat wheat, or try it instead of a traditional cake.

Ingredients
175g (6oz) polyunsaturated margarine
125g (4oz) soft dark brown sugar
30ml (2 tbsp) clear honey
2 eggs, beaten
45ml (3 tbsp) orange juice
45ml (3 tbsp) sherry or brandy
225g (8oz) raisins
50g (2oz) glacé fruits, quartered
50g (2oz) almonds, chopped
225g (8oz) rye flour
125g (4oz) oat flour
5ml (1 tsp) cinnamon
2.5ml (½ tsp) nutmeg

Equipment
20-cm (8-in) round cake tin (pan), greased and lined
mixing bowl
wooden spoon or electric mixer
metal spoon
wire cooling rack

Heat the oven to 160°C (325°F) Gas Mark 3. Place the margarine and sugar in the mixing bowl and beat together until light and fluffy – this should take about 5 minutes. Mix together the honey, eggs, orange juice and brandy, then beat them into the creamed mixture, adding a little at a time, until they are all incorporated. Stir in the raisins, glacé fruits and almonds. Mix together the flours and spices, then gently fold them into the mixture until all the ingredients are thoroughly combined. Transfer the mixture to the prepared tin (pan) and press down firmly. Smooth the top with the back of the metal spoon. Bake for 1¼-1½ hours until the cake is firm to the touch and well-browned. Allow to cool in the tin for 20 minutes, then turn out, remove the lining paper and leave on the wire rack until cold.

Eggless fruit cake

Once made, this cake is best stored in the fridge, because it doesn't keep for long.

Ingredients
225g (8oz) currants
225g (8oz) raisins
225g (8oz) sultanas
450ml (¾ pint) apple juice
140ml (¼ pint) sunflower oil
350g (12oz) wholemeal self-raising flour
50g (2oz) blanched almonds, chopped
15ml (1 tbsp) black treacle
5ml (1 tsp) finely-grated lemon rind
5ml (1 tsp) mixed spice
5ml (1 tsp) ground cinnamon
75g (3oz) dark brown sugar

Equipment
20-cm (8-in) round cake tin (pan), greased and lined
mixing bowl
wooden spoon or electric mixer
metal spoon
wire cooling rack

Heat the oven to 150°C (300°F) Gas Mark 2. Place all the ingredients in the mixing bowl, stir well to mix, then beat them together for 2-3 minutes until well amalgamated. Transfer to the prepared tin (pan) and smooth the top with the back of the metal spoon. Bake for 1¾-2 hours until well-browned and firm to the touch. Allow to cool in the tin, then turn out onto a wire cooling rack and remove the lining paper. Leave until cold.

Wholefood sandwich cake

If you don't eat ordinary sponge and sandwich cakes because you believe they aren't healthy, try this one instead.

Ingredients
175g (6oz) self-raising wholemeal flour
175g (6oz) soft light brown sugar
175g (6oz) polyunsaturated margarine
3 free-range eggs
4.5ml (1½ tsp) baking powder
extra-fruit jam, buttercream or whipped cream

Equipment
2 20-cm (8-in) round sandwich tins (pans), greased and lined
mixing bowl
wooden spoon or electric mixer
small knife
wire cooling racks

Heat the oven to 160°C (325°F) Gas Mark 3. Place all the ingredients in the mixing bowl and beat together to mix, then beat for a further 2-3 minutes (1-2 minutes if using an electric mixer) until the mixture is light and fluffy. Divide the mixture between the two prepared tins (pans) and smooth the tops. Bake for 30-35 minutes until golden brown and springy to the touch. Loosen the edges of the cakes with your fingers or a small knife, then turn out onto a wire cooling rack. Remove the lining paper and leave until cold, then sandwich the cakes together with extra-fruit jam, buttercream or whipped cream.

BREAD PONY

Ingredients
1 small granary or wholemeal loaf (for body)
5 oblong granary or wholemeal rolls
(for legs and head)
1 long granary or wholemeal French stick
2 candied lemon slices
ends of a breadstick
1 pretzel ring
handful of thick pretzel sticks
watercress
radish roses

Equipment
bread knife
bread board
cocktail sticks (wooden toothpicks)

Attach the legs first. Place the loaf for the body with the rounded side uppermost, and push two cocktail sticks (wooden toothpicks) into each corner. Push one bread roll on each pair of cocktail sticks, then turn over to stand up on its legs. If the rolls are not identical in size, trim them so that the pony stands without support. Cut the French stick at an angle to make the neck rest flat on the body. Attach with cocktail sticks. To make the pony's face, slice triangles from the French stick for ears. The eyes are lemon slices with pupils made from the ends of bread sticks, held in place with cocktail sticks, and the nose is a pretzel ring fixed in position with a cocktail stick. Fasten the head to the neck with cocktail sticks. Cut two small pieces for the haunches and fasten to the back legs, then finish with the ends of the French stick. The tail is made by attaching the pretzel sticks to the back. Place the pony in a field of watercress, decorated with radish roses.

Decorating breads

Decorative bread figures make charming centrepieces for children's parties or buffet tables, and they are very quick and easy to make. The wide selection of types, shapes and sizes of bread and rolls available makes it easy to plan and create dozens of different figures.

To make a crocodile, use a long French stick for the body, with one end sliced open for the mouth. Slice a roll in four to make the legs. Add olives for eyes and carrot teeth.

To make a camel, follow the instructions for the pony, but make small round ears and a shorter tail. Cut a small round roll in half and position on the back for the humps.

To make a teddy bear, use a round loaf for the body and a smaller round roll for the head. Cut an oblong roll in four to make the arms and legs. Decorate the face with vegetable pieces, or pipe on features made from coloured cream cheese.

To make a panda bear, follow the instructions for the teddy bear, using white bread for the body and head, and wholemeal or pumpernickel rolls for the arms, legs, snout and ears.

To make a caterpillar, assemble a train of small bread rolls, then add pretzel antennae and vegetable pieces for the face.

If the bread figure is to be served at a children's party, it is a good idea to cut the bread and carefully remove all the cocktail sticks before serving.

SAVOURY SANDWICH

Ingredients
1 large wholemeal or granary loaf
700g (1½lb) cream cheese
50g (2oz) grated Cheddar cheese
1 small carrot, grated
4 hardboiled eggs
30ml (2 tbsp) mayonnaise
2 boxes mustard and cress
15ml (1 tbsp) tomato purée
1 large red pepper (capsicum), diced
1 large yellow pepper (capsicum), diced
cherry tomatoes
pretzels
salt and freshly-ground pepper

Equipment
carving knife
bread board
mixing bowls
fork
knife
large fabric or plastic piping bag
large star or shell nozzle

Slice the bread in four horizontally. Mix together 350g (12oz) cream cheese with the Cheddar cheese and grated carrot, season to taste then put to one side. Mash the hardboiled eggs with the mayonnaise, season to taste and set aside. Mix the tomato purée with the remaining cream cheese, season to taste and set to one side. Build up the loaf by spreading most of the tomato and cheese mixture on the bottom layer. Scatter lots of diced pepper (capsicum) over the top. Spread a thick layer of egg mayonnaise on the second slice of bread and cover this with most of the mustard and cress. Spread most of the cream cheese and carrot mixture on the third slice of bread, then stack the layers on top of each other, finishing with the fourth slice. Carefully cover this with the remainder of the cream cheese mixtures, piped if you wish. Place the loaf on a plate or board and garnish with the peppers, mustard and cress, cherry tomatoes and pretzels. To cut the loaf, hold it in position with a carving fork and slice with a sharp carving knife.

PARTY PIZZAS

Dough
450g (1lb) wholewheat flour
10ml (2 tsp) yeast
340ml (12 fl oz) hand-hot water
5ml (1 tsp) salt
5ml (1 tsp) sugar
pepper to taste

Topping
800g (1lb 12oz) tinned tomatoes, chopped
1 medium onion, sliced
15ml (1 tbsp) oil
1 clove garlic, crushed
5ml (1 tsp) mixed herbs

Decoration
1 tin anchovies, drained
1 small piece mozzarella, cut into stars or crescents
5 slices salami, cut into decorative shapes
few slices of cucumber
few stuffed olives, sliced

Equipment
baking tray, greased
mixing bowl, warmed
metal whisk
large jug
scissors
clean tea towel
frying pan
wooden spoon
large flat tray

Mix together the flour, salt and pepper in the warmed bowl. Measure the water into a jug, whisk in the sugar and then the yeast. Leave to stand for about 10 minutes. Once this mixture has developed a large frothy head, stir it into the dry ingredients and mix into a smooth dough. Turn onto a floured board and knead. Press the dough onto the greased baking tray and form into a Christmas tree shape, using scissors to cut out the points of the branches. Make parcels from the scraps of left-over dough, then cover them all with a clean tea towel and leave in a warm place until the dough has risen. Heat the oven to 200°C (400°F) Gas Mark 6. To make the topping, place the oil in the frying pan, add the onions and garlic and cook on a medium heat until the onion is transparent. Add the tomatoes and herbs and simmer, stirring continually, until most of the liquid has evaporated to leave a thick pulp. Remove from the heat and set aside. Uncover the pizzas, spoon the tomato pulp onto the dough and decorate with the salami and mozzarella. Cut the anchovies in half lengthwise and place diagonally on the tree to form tinsel. Arrange the remaining scraps of anchovy in crosses on the parcels to represent string, and decorate with sliced olives. Place the pizzas in the oven and bake for 30 minutes, checking the parcels after 15 minutes. When the pizzas are ready, place on a large flat tray and garnish with halved slices of cucumber.

Making small pizzas

You can make individual pizzas using the same dough and topping mixtures, but instead of making a Christmas tree, cut the dough into novelty shapes such as stars, baby Christmas trees, circles, crescent moons, triangles, ovals or the initials of each of your guests. The pizzas should be cooked at the same temperature as the large Christmas tree, but allow only 15-20 minutes cooking time.

PRINTED IN BELGIUM BY
proost
INTERNATIONAL BOOK PRODUCTS